T0329217

Cambridge Elements ≡

Elements in Religion and Violence
edited by
James R. Lewis
University of Tromsø
Margo Kitts
Hawai'i Pacific University

TIBETAN DEMONOLOGY

Christopher Bell
Stetson University

CAMBRIDGE
UNIVERSITY PRESS

CAMBRIDGE
UNIVERSITY PRESS

University Printing House, Cambridge CB2 8BS, United Kingdom

One Liberty Plaza, 20th Floor, New York, NY 10006, USA

477 Williamstown Road, Port Melbourne, VIC 3207, Australia

314–321, 3rd Floor, Plot 3, Splendor Forum, Jasola District Centre,
New Delhi – 110025, India

79 Anson Road, #06–04/06, Singapore 079906

Cambridge University Press is part of the University of Cambridge.

It furthers the University's mission by disseminating knowledge in the pursuit of
education, learning, and research at the highest international levels of excellence.

www.cambridge.org
Information on this title: www.cambridge.org/9781108712675
DOI: 10.1017/9781108670715

First published 2020

A catalogue record for this publication is available from the British Library.

ISBN 978-1-108-71267-5 Paperback
ISSN 2397-9496 (online)
ISSN 2514-3786 (print)

Tibetan Demonology

Elements in Religion and Violence

DOI: 10.1017/9781108670715

First published online: June 2020

Christopher Bell

Stetson University

Author for correspondence: Christopher Bell, cbell@stetson.edu

ABSTRACT: *Tibetan Demonology* discusses the rich taxonomy of gods and demons encountered in Tibet. These spirits are often the cause of, and exhorted for, diverse violent and wrathful activities. This Element consists of four thematic sections. The first section, "Spirits and the Body," explores oracular possession and spirit-induced illnesses. The second section, "Spirits and Time," discusses the role of gods in Tibetan astrology and ritual calendars. The third section, "Spirits and Space," examines the relationship between divinities and the Tibetan landscape. The final section, "Spirits and Doctrine," explores how certain deities act as fierce protectors of religious and political institutions.

KEYWORDS: Tibet, demonology, ritual, demons, gods

ISBNs: 9781108712675 (PB), 9781108670715 (OC)

ISSNs: 2397-9496 (online), 2514-3786 (print)

Contents

Introduction   1

I Spirits and the Body   19

II Spirits and Time   36

III Spirits and Space   46

IV Spirits and Doctrine   55

Conclusion   64

Tibetan Transliteration and Translation   72

Glossary   73

Bibliography   81

Introduction

The Tibetan plateau may seem sparse, but it is overrun with the lives, adventures, and influences of innumerable gods and demons. These beings play a significant role in shaping the religious history of Tibet and continue to have a strong presence in the daily practices and worship of Tibetans. Such entities are elicited in every facet of Tibetan cultural history. If a king is oppressing Buddhism, as in the case of Lang Darma in the ninth century, he is believed to be possessed by a demon, and thus must be subjugated (i.e., assassinated). Conversely, the Tibetan Buddhist kings were believed to be possessed by demons by practitioners of Bön, who were being persecuted in the seventh and eighth centuries. The Tibetan people believe themselves to be descended from gods and demons from various heavenly realms, as well as from emanations of the bodhisattvas Avalokiteśvara and Tārā. The Tibetan landscape is thought to be teeming with spirits, which is the explanation given for the plateau's harsh environment. The very land is said to be a giant reclining demoness who was subjugated by temples constructed by the first Tibetan Buddhist king, Songtsen Gampo (557/617–650). A popular narrative trope in Tibetan ritual and mythic literature is of the eighth-century tantric master Padmasambhava exorcising and converting indigenous spirits of the land to Buddhism, often through destructive means. Tibetan medical texts describe the various demonic species that cause numerous kinds of ailments, and how to expel them in the process of healing. To this day, gods and demons play a strong pragmatic role in the daily and annual rituals of both Buddhist and Bön, lay and monastic, communities.

A common thread in these various interactions with Tibetan spirits is that they are generally capricious and violent. They are often blamed for illnesses, considered harbingers of misfortune or karmic consequences, and can even kill as an act of retribution or by stealing an individual's soul. Anyone can fall victim to such violence, but it can also be quelled, harnessed, or directed by ritual specialists, and even interpreted toward soteriological ends. Part of containing or channeling the violence of Tibetan gods and spirits requires identifying and categorizing them in relation to one another. This is no easy task. Tibetans have at best developed loosely systematic spirit typologies and ontologies in an attempt to cope with the dizzying assortment of nonhuman agents,[1] drawing from both Indian and indigenous taxonomies. More specifically, distinct Tibetan religious lineages and even individual masters have developed their own pantheons of divinities. In collected works and monastic ritual catalogs, these pantheons evince a hierarchy ranging from enlightened beings and tantric deities emulated to achieve enlightenment, to guardian deities converted to Buddhism and entreated for protection, and finally to local demonic beings warded off with apotropaic rites. This spectrum of nonhuman beings also makes it difficult to establish clear boundaries between transcendent beings that fit more comfortably under the label of soteriological divinities and those spirits better classified under demonology. The problem is further exacerbated by many such beings having once been living historical figures, and by several spirit terms referencing the divine origins of past Tibetan kings.[2]

The term "demon" has become popular in the secondary literature that refers to these beings, given their general penchant for pernicious activity. This is problematic because of the linguistic difficulty inherent in representing these various spirit classes with limited English vocabulary. While English has one overarching term for demons, there are numerous kinds of nonhuman agents that exist in Tibet, possessing vastly different attributes and qualities both beneficent and malevolent. There has been much scholarly debate on the utility of "demon" in Greek, Egyptian, Israelite, and early Christian religious contexts. In his exploration of the original Greek term *daimon* and its later Roman usages, Jonathan Z. Smith understands demons as ultimately liminal beings and the demonic as a locative and relational category that helps define boundaries. Through ritual action the "demon is 'placed' by being named, entrapped and removed to its proper realm (e.g. exorcism) or redirected to a 'proper' goal (i.e. to somewhere or someone else, as in so-called 'hostile' magic)."[3] In his work on Tibetan spirits, Cameron Bailey uses the Greek term in hopes of recapturing its original breadth of usage, though he acknowledges that it does not completely

---

[1] I use the term nonhuman to refer to these spirits and their activities rather than the etic term "supernatural." Tibetans believe that these beings are as much a part of the world as humans are, and are not thought to transcend nature but to exist within it.

[2] See Karmay 2003, pp. 69, 71, and Karmay 1998b, pp. 294–305.

[3] Smith 1978, pp. 428–429.

map onto the Indo-Tibetan context.[4] Others have attempted to recognize the individuality of these diverse spirit types by using European nonhuman terminology. For instance, the spirit type called *tsen* has been translated as "furies," while *sinpo* spirits have been called "orcs," "ogres," and "gnomes."[5] While it is admirable to use distinct terms for each spirit, these etic labels also carry specific cultural connotations and convey characteristics that are not true to the original Tibetan concepts. A *sinpo* looks very different from the popular images of gnomes. Due to the various limitations of the above attempts at translating individual spirit types, it is ultimately best to render them phonetically. While initially cumbersome, this method has the benefit of using emic terminology for such distinct indigenous concepts. When discussing these beings, I continue to use the term "demon," though more when referring to certain Tibetan spirits who are considered especially violent and harmful in nature. I use the broader term "spirit" more frequently, which speaks to the original nature of many of these beings as the restless spirits of past individuals.

The goal of this Element is to act as an introduction to Tibetan demonology, providing a brief overview of its primary structures, classifications, content, and scholarship, especially as they pertain to various kinds of violence, so that the informed and interested reader can explore deeper avenues of this robust topic. With a field of inquiry that could easily fill multiple volumes, let alone a short one like this, the focus of this work is inevitably on taxonomy, categorization, and summary. Nevertheless, it is important to be cognizant of the greater complexities and multivocalities hiding beneath and behind the illusory order presented. In his extensive exploration of Japanese pantheons – or what he more accurately describes as "polytheons"[6] – Bernard Faure discusses the pitfalls of essentializing narratives while recognizing the need to occasionally fallback on accessible language for the sake of expediency. In describing Japanese divinities and their relation to the human communities in which they are found, Faure draws on the actor–network theory developed by Bruno Latour, Michel Callon, and

---

[4] Bailey 2012, pp. 11–12.

[5] These definitions can be found in the Rangjung Yeshe Tibetan-English Dictionary of Buddhist Culture, now searchable online; see Rangjung Yeshe Wiki 2018.

[6] See Faure 2016, p. 13.

John Law. The notion of actor–network emphasizes the relationships between human and nonhuman actors creating constantly shifting constellations of strategic interaction and intersection. As such, gods and demons are active agents as much as humans are, signifying equally important nodes in a larger network. Faure describes the Japanese gods succinctly in their capacity to act and change across personal and social contexts:

> The gods are multilevel, kaleidoscopic phenomena (some would say *noumena* and *numina*): they exist both at the level of individual belief and at that of collective representations. At the level of society, they represent larger forces, institutions, or groups, which are often in conflict: temples, shrines, lineages, palaces, courtiers, warriors, itinerant priests and artists, Yin-Yang Masters, and so on.[7]

With some variation, this description could apply to the multivalent and often convoluted interactions between humans and nonhumans in the Tibetan milieu. Regardless, the following organization and taxonomic descriptions are meant to offer a limited but necessary demonological grammar upon which deeper reflection and scholarly exploration can advance.

Tibetan Demonologies

The difficulties and caveats of translation and organization aside, attempting to delimit and consolidate Tibetan demonology is still a valuable enterprise. Jonathan Z. Smith notes that taxonomy can help to clarify the shifting perspectives of the demonic – which he calls chaotic and protean – that nonetheless are presented in seemingly ordered systems within a culture (or cultures) across time and between regions. His observation that devotees themselves are "obsessed" with making distinctions and categories can certainly be observed in the examples below.[8] As Rita Lucarelli explains, the use of "demonology" as a starting point for exploration, as well as a comparative exercise, is "useful in order to give a descriptive basis to analysis, stimulating issues of definition,

---

[7] Faure 2016, p. 14.

[8] See Smith 1978, pp. 437–438. I use "devotee" in place of the now obsolete and offensive "primitive" that Smith uses, though, he seems to have been aware of its negative shift in connotation at the time.

classification, religious and social function of demons and their interaction with humankind."[9] Bruce Lincoln likewise considers the concept a fruitful lens through which to explore the cultural intersections of threatening categories that are otherwise approached separately in the West, such as epidemiology, teratology, and criminology.[10] Demonological schemes and catalogs are also found in the cultures surrounding the Tibetan plateau, such as Indian *bhūtavidyā* literature or Chinese apotropaic manuals such as the *Album of the White Marsh*.[11] For their part, Tibetans have themselves attempted, with only partial success, to classify their spirit types. One could perhaps more accurately speak of "demonologies" rather than a singular Tibetan demonology.

The earliest and most common Tibetan classification scheme for spirit types is the "Eight Classes of Gods and Serpent Spirits" (*lhalu degyé*) or "Eight Classes of Gods and Flesh-eating Spirits" (*lhasin degyé*), which are often used synonymously despite their different wording. The former expression appears in Dunhuang documents but does not enumerate what these eight spirit types are. However, a ninth-century Tibetan translation of the *Golden Light Sutra* (*Suvarṇaprabhāsasūtra*) offers a list of eight spirits, presented here with their Sanskrit equivalents:

1. *lha* (*deva*)

2. *lu* (*nāga*)

3. *nöjin* (*yakṣa*)

4. *driʒa* (*gandharva*)

5. *lhamayin* (*asura*)

6. *kyung* (*garuḍa*)

7. *miamchi* (*kimnara*)

8. *tochechenpo* (*mahoraga*)[12]

---

[9] Lucarelli 2013, p. 22. Another valuable exploration in defining "demon" and "demonology" is Frankfurter 2012.

[10] Lincoln 2012, p. 31. I am grateful to Matthew Goff for drawing my attention to this work.

[11] See, respectively, Smith 2006, pp. 472–530, and von Glahn 2004, pp. 84–91. For more on Indian demonology, see Bhattacharyya 2000. For more on the origins and development of Chinese demonographical and demonological literature, see Harper 1985.

[12] See Karmay 2003, p. 73.

Not surprisingly this list is Buddhist in orientation, offering the Tibetan equivalents of popular Indian deities and spirits rather than indigenous categories.[13] By the fourteenth century, the list had not only taken on greater Tibetan characteristics but also came to include several levels. In keeping with common tantric doxographic practices,[14] the *Chronicle of Gods and Demons* lists eight outer, inner, and secret classes of gods and flesh-eating spirits (*lhamasin degyé*).[15] The eight outer classes are: (1) *gongpo*, (2) *teurang*, (3) *denma*, (4) *sadak*, (5) *yülha*, (6) *men*, (7) *tsen*, and (8) *lu*. The eight inner classes are: (1) *sokdak*, (2) *mamo*, (3) *shinjé*, (4) *dü*, (5) *nöjin*, (6) *mu*, (7) *dralha*, and (8) *gongpo*. Finally, the eight secret classes refer to the planetary deities: (1) *Jitripatra*, (2) *Jangöndrakpo*, (3) *Duwajukring*, (4) *Barrarotsa*, (5) *Drashenjin*, (6) *Jinuratsa*, (7) *Rāhula*, and (8) *Kyapjukchenpo*.[16]

As Samten Karmay notes, while the authority of the Indian Buddhist list continued to be acknowledged, Tibetan categories became more prevalent. This is evinced in the work of the eighteenth-century Geluk master Longdöl Ngawang Lozang (1719–1794), who composed one of the most extensive and organized demonologies for Tibetan deities and spirit types. In this work, he describes the eight gods and spirits as follows:

1. the white *lha*
2. the red *tsen*
3. the black *dü*
4. the multicolored *ẓa*
5. the brown *mu*
6. the flesh-eating *sinpo*

---

[13] For an extensive exploration of the interplay between trans-Buddhist deities and Indo-Tibetan spirits, see Ruegg 2008.

[14] For instance, see Dalton 2005.

[15] See Karmay 2003, p. 75. In this variant Tibetan spelling, the negative *ma* is placed between *lha* and *sin*, and would be literally understood as "neither gods nor flesh-eating spirits." However, in this context it is better understood as "both gods and flesh-eating spirits," and so is synonymous with the aforementioned *lhasin*.

[16] See Blondeau 1971, pp. 109–110. For the original, see O rgyan gling pa 1997, pp. 75–83.

7. *gyelpo*, the wealth lords
8. *mamo*, the disease mistresses[17]

While variations still exist, by modern times greater iconographic detail has been added to these spirits in an effort to standardize their categorization and representation. Françoise Pommaret offers the following description of the eight gods and spirits as they were relayed to her by the chant master of Lhodrak Kharchu Monastery in Bhutan, where they are illustrated on murals:

1. *lha*: mounted on a white yak, this is an armored warrior brandishing a sword.
2. *gyelpo*: mounted on a snow lion, this is a monk wearing a flat-brimmed hat and holding a bowl filled with grains and a mendicant's staff with bells.
3. *lu*: mounted on a sea serpent (*makara*), this is a half-human, half-serpent being holding a bag of diseases.
4. *nöjin*: mounted on a tiger, this is a terrifying black being holding a sword and jewel.
5. *dü*: mounted on a black ox, this is a terrifying black being holding a wooden score stick and a small sacrificial cake.
6. *mamo*: mounted on a dragon, this is a terrifying white being holding a mirror and an arrow adorned with a silken scarf.
7. *tsen*: mounted on a horse, this is a black being wearing armor and holding a bow and arrows.
8. *Mu*: mounted on a mule, this is a terrifying black being holding a wooden score stick and a black banner.[18]

Clearly the order and composition of these spirit catalogs changes depending on the text and time period.[19] Other systems have tried to integrate these spirits more fully into Buddhist cosmology by assigning each spirit type to one or more of the six Buddhist realms of rebirth. For instance, *lu* spirits belong to both the god and animal realms, while *nöjin* reside firmly in the god realm.[20] As Ronald

---

[17] Ngag dbang blo bzang 1991, p. 485. See also Karmay 2003, p. 74.
[18] Pommaret 2003a, p. 46.
[19] For other examples see Nebesky-Wojkowitz 1998, pp. 253–317, and Tucci 1999, vol. 2, pp. 717–730.
[20] These classifications can be found, for instance, in the Rangjung Yeshe Tibetan-English Dictionary.

Davidson has observed, most of these deities were initially indigenous and only later assimilated into Indian Buddhist and tantric classification systems, yet they still retained many of their Tibetan attributes.[21] Decades earlier, René de Nebesky-Wojkowitz made a similar observation when discussing the Tibetan names for the Indian gods Indra (*Gyajin*) and Brahmā (*Tsangpa*). In certain Tibetan texts these names appear to refer to groups of autochthonous spirits or otherwise regional deities.[22] Although Buddhist rhetoric treats the related Indic type as synonymous with their equivalent Tibetan terms, there are significant cultural differences between them. Certain texts speak more to the Indian versions of these spirits than to the Tibetan, and negotiations between Sanskrit and indigenous representations have been taking place since the imperial era.

Regardless, these hybrid lists are generally the product of religious professionals placing a patina of organization over organically shifting and regionally specific terms and concepts. Interwoven within these categorization schemes are territorially distinct spirits with deep cultural roots. Using Ladakh as their field site, both Sophie Day and Martin Mills note the triple-tiered cosmology commonly found across the Himalayas and the Tibetan Plateau. This system divides the world into the realm above, inhabited by the *lha*; the middle realm, where the warlike *tsen* prowl; and the world below, where the *lu* reside.[23] In contrast to the Bhutanese description of *tsen* above, Mills notes that in Ladakh they are perceived as "half-beings who lack backs, and wander the roads at the edge of the village during the twilight hours, occasionally stealing the life-force (*sparkha*) of new-born children."[24] Around Tibet's Northern Plains (*Changtang*), it is the *nyen* spirit who is the denizen of the middle realm;[25] and yet for Kagyü ritualists in Eastern Tibet (*Kham*), the *nyen* reside in the realm above while the *sadak* reside in the middle.[26] Regional variations aside, the tripartite cosmology and the spirits who inhabit it are intimately tied to village and household spatial structuring.[27] Charles Ramble notes that such innumerable local variations make a universal and comprehensive classification

---

[21] Davidson 2005, p. 217. [22] See Nebesky-Wojkowitz 1998, pp. 99–100, 145.
[23] See Day 1989, pp. 58–64, and Mills 2003, pp. 151–164. [24] Mills 2003, p. 151.
[25] See Bellezza 2011, p. 11. [26] See Beyer 1978, p. 294.
[27] See Mills 2003, pp. 153–161.

scheme impossible, since how spirits are approached or understood in practice deviates markedly from textual descriptions. He further argues that "it may be that gods of place are associated with distinctive categories of activity not just insofar as they are individuals, or belong to classes, but to the extent that they form different configurations."[28] Spirit typologies are ultimately less important than how a spirit's role and function shift in accordance to their relation to the varying needs of the community. For instance, Ramble sees this network of relationships along vertical and horizontal axes, where local spirits act as bringers of rain, wealth, and abundance on a vertical plane and as defenders of the territory on a horizontal one. The various contexts of these geometric configurations are elicited depending on whether the deity is invoked through offerings, oracular possessions, or songs.[29] The positionality of these spirits is always connected to other spirit types and the human community in an ever-changing constellation of relationships.

Other overlapping indigenous demonological categories and types exist that were later incorporated into larger Buddhist and Bön contexts and corpora. For example, there are the "Nine Masang Brothers" (*masang püngu*) who ruled over the territories of Tibet. Treated as singular beings rather than spirit types, these brothers are: *nöjin, dü, sinpo, lu, tsen, lha, mu, dre,* and *gongpo*.[30] These and other brother groups are the subject of numerous stories, and especially permeate the rich oral and textual literature of the Gesar epic.[31] There are also the "Five Personal Gods" (*gowé lhanga*) that are believed to be born with every individual to act as their protectors. These divinities are described in predominantly Bön texts, but are also found in Buddhist sources, including the famous *Songs of Milarepa*. They include the "father god" (*polha*), "mother god" (*malha*), "maternal uncle god" (*zhanglha*), "enemy god" (*dralha*), and "life god" (*soklha*).[32] There are minor variations of

---

[28] Ramble 1996, p. 141.   [29] See Ramble 2008, pp. 195–202.
[30] See Tucci 1999, vol. 2, p. 717, and Beyer 1978, pp. 292–301.
[31] The recently published English translation of the Epic of Gesar is full of numerous examples; see Kornman, et al. 2015.
[32] See Jovic 2010, especially pp. 12–17. See also Berounský 2007 and Dotson 2017.

this list as well.[33] There is also the nebulous label "Arrogant Ones" (*drekpa*), which predominantly refers to lower ranking spirits in the retinues of higher deities, but it can also reference individuals.[34] There is even a classification scheme of a thousand gods and demons, according to one Nyingma tantra examined by Anne-Marie Blondeau.[35] Tibetans continue to make such lists of spirit types varying in number, length, and detail.[36]

Spirit Typologies

There is a great deal of overlap and variation between these demonologies. Tibetan spirit types have multivalent and even contradictory characteristics, and some are notably more frequent in appearance than others. Taxonomic labels such as *lha*, *tsen*, and *nöjin* appear in several diverse contexts, while *denma* and *men* are much scarcer and their descriptions relatively vague.[37] Moreover, for other spirit types in these lists, there is some ambiguity in their usage as to whether they refer to a specific race of nonhuman beings or reflect a title of office. For instance, *sadak*, *zhidak*, and *yülha* are often used to refer to the local land deity, valley deity, or mountain deity, whatever their specific type or name may be otherwise.[38] It is also quite common for individual deities to belong to multiple spirit types at once. For example, the Buddhist protector deity Tsiu Marpo is by turns called a *tsen* and a *nöjin*. Finally, there are several other common spirit types that do not appear in these lists at all, or which only occasionally appear in ritual texts. These spirits, such as *kula* and *dri*, are predominantly found in Dunhuang texts, have either faded or come about in later usage, or have shifted considerably in meaning over time.[39]

---

[33] See Nebesky-Wojkowitz 1998, pp. 327–328. [34] See Ibid, pp. 253–317.

[35] See Blondeau 2008.

[36] For a modern example, Ben Joffe has translated the second chapter of an anti-Dorjé Shukden Tibetan polemic published in 2006 that describes 28 distinct spirit types; see Joffe 2016.

[37] For some discussion of the latter term, see Nebesky-Wojkowitz 1998, pp. 181–183, 198–202, and Stein 1939.

[38] See Nebesky-Wojkowitz 1998, pp. 203–230, and Heller 1996, pp. 138–139.

[39] The classification of *kula* as a mountain deity has especially been the subject of much scholarly debate; see Macdonald 1971, Blondeau 1976, pp. 241–242,

Despite these numerous differences and exceptions, it is helpful to give concise definitions for the spirit types most often encountered in Tibetan religious literature and practice, as well as the common characteristics or iconographies they possess. In sharp contrast to the standardizing attempts above to limit the list to eight spirits, I offer here two dozen terms – which are still not comprehensive – in an attempt at breadth and depth. While the earlier categorization schemes appear to be an admixture of Buddhist and indigenous hierarchies, I have chosen to list the spirit types alphabetically for ease of reference:[40]

- *dön*: While generally malicious spirits, *dön* are closely associated with epilepsy as well as maladies that afflict children. The most famous group of *dön* refers to fifteen such spirits that endanger children.[41]
- *dralha*: These spirits are autochthonous Tibetan deities and often appear as decorated warriors on horseback. Literally, this word could be translated as "enemy god"; however, these deities are usually portrayed as allies who defeat one's enemies. Todd Gibson argues that these spirits started off as muses; the term was originally spelled *sgra lha*, meaning "voice god," and refers to the spirits speaking into a poet's ear.[42]
- *dre*: This is a fairly common term for demonic spirits, though one with several subcategories. As Géza Bethlenfalvy explains, "The malicious dre demons

Pommaret 1996, Karmay 1998h, Karmay 2003, pp. 68–69, Walter 2009, pp. 97–196, and Hill 2015. For *si* spirits and subtypes, see Nebesky-Wojkowitz 1998, pp. 299–303, Kohn 2001, pp. 79–81, Sihlé 2002, and Ramble 2017. For *dri*, see Karmay 2003, p. 70.

[40] The main sources used to compile this list are Bethlenfalvy 2003; Beyer 1978, pp. 293–301; Cornu 2002, pp. 247–253; Reb gong pa 2009, pp. 53–122; Samuel 1993, pp. 162–163 (translated from Cornu 1990, pp. 226–229); and Tucci 1999, vol. 2, pp. 717–730. For extensive catalogs and iconographic depictions of these and other related spirit types, see Farkas and Szabó 2002, Kelényi 2003, and Watt 2019. While originally published more than a century ago, Waddell 1973 (pp. 136–177) also explores Tibetan demonology, and in tandem with astrology, which will be discussed later. For a Bön categorization scheme, see Achard 2003.

[41] See Lin 2013 and Sárközi 2012.

[42] See Gibson 1985, Nebesky-Wojkowitz 1998, pp. 318–340, and Forgues 2017. See Berounský 2009 for an alternative etiology.

are grouped into a class of five, of whom the *ẕa'dre* [*ẕadre*] demons cause problems deriving from food; the *god'dre* [*gödre*] demons cause various losses and ill-luck; the *gshed'dre* [*shédre*] are executioners torturing beings in the [Buddhist] hell; the *chu'dre* [*chudre*] cause the illnesses that come from water; while the *gson'dre* [*söndre*] demons cause material loss."[43]

- *dü*: These spirits are also openly malevolent and create hindrances, usually to prevent the completion of rituals or success on the path to enlightenment. They are generally black in color and are said to have opposed the Buddhist teachings in their past lives. The associated Sanskrit word is *Māra*, referring to the god who personifies *saṃsāra* and attempted but failed to hinder the enlightenment of the historical Buddha Śākyamuni. Along with the words *dön* and *dre*, this word comes closest to generically refer to "demons" in Tibetan texts.

- *gek*: These are obstacle-inducing spirits that also hinder ritual success like the *dü*. They are often presented in a pair with human enemies (*dra*), being formless villains in contrast to corporeal ones.

- *gyelpo*: The name of these spirits literally means "king," since many such beings were powerful kings in their past lives. The mythic accounts for most of these spirits claim that they were once kings or monks who transgressed their religious vows. They are generally white in color.

- *jungpo, yidak*: The *jungpo* spirits refer to ghosts generically, while *yidak* are hungry ghosts (Skt. *preta*), referring specifically to the denizens of one of the six realms of rebirth in traditional Buddhist cosmology. Hungry ghosts are a vague and mutable category across different forms of Buddhism, with their iconography and characteristics often reflecting the culture into which they have been assimilated.

- *kandroma* (Skt. *ḍākinī*): These important deities were adopted from Indian tantric cosmology. *Kandroma* are a class of ancient female beings found in the entourages of all major tantric Buddhist deities. They fill the intermediate spaces of *maṇḍalas*, are messengers and inspirers of Buddhist scripture, and signify pervasive wisdom, which is personified as feminine in Mahāyāna Buddhism. As such, *kandroma* are involved in all major Tibetan Buddhist ritual processes and can be invoked for

[43] Bethlenfalvy 2003, p. 38.

protective purposes; they are also fierce guardians of religious texts.[44] These deities have a male equivalent (*kandro*; Skt. *ḍāka*), but they are not nearly as popular in Tibetan Buddhism.

- *lha*: This term is used to refer to celestial beings that inhabit the highest of the six realms of rebirth in Buddhist cosmology. However, in Tibetan texts this term's usage often more generically refers to nonhuman spiritual beings overall, even tantric deities, much like the term "god" in English. Michael Walter argues that the earliest Tibetan usage of *lha*, dating to the imperial age, denoted the deceased ancestors of rulers and high officials. The term was frequently used as a collective reference to these spirits in hopes of securing their blessings and protection.[45]

- *lu*: These are serpentine deities who generally abide in lakes, rivers, and subterranean realms. They are known to pollute water and hinder the construction of dykes and irrigation works. If angered, they can bring about diseases such as leprosy. Common iconography shows these spirits as having a human head and torso, and a snake's tail instead of legs. This is due to heavy Buddhist influence, however, and earlier accounts suggest a dramatically different appearance. For instance, in a famous biography of the Bön founder Shenrap Miwo, a black *lu* is described as having 360 spider-like limbs and a single eye in its forehead, with poison dripping from its mouth.[46] Tibetan medical texts likewise describe these chthonic spirits as taking on diverse animal forms, such as frogs, scorpions, and spiders.[47]

- *mamo*: These are illness-bringing goddesses who are pictured "as ugly women with long, emaciated breasts and huge sexual organs, while only a few are said to have the lovely appearance of 'a girl who has just passed

---

[44] See Snellgrove 2002, pp. 167–168, and Beyer 1978, pp. 45–47, 399. See also Herrmann-Pfandt 1992–1993, Germano and Gyatso 2000, and Simmer-Brown 2001.

[45] For more on the complex social, political, and religious conceptions of *lha* in imperial Tibet, see Walter 2009, pp. 110–123.

[46] Francke 1930, p. 18. For an extensive anthropological exploration of the *lu* cult in Ladakh, see Niermann 2008. I would like to thank Diana Lange for drawing my attention to this text.

[47] See Vargas-O'Bryan 2013, p. 107.

her sixteenth year of age'."[48] The protector deity Penden Lhamo is considered the chief of the *mamo* spirits.[49]

- *mu*: These spirits are somewhat obscure, though they are considered to be very ancient Tibetan deities. They are extremely savage and noxious in nature, and cause dropsy and drought. One of the primeval clans of Tibet was also called *mu*.[50]

- *nöjin*: These spirits were initially malicious beings that caused diseases and epidemics. In order to signify their later conversion to guardians of the Buddhist teachings, they have become associated with the ancient Indian spirits called *yakṣas*.[51] As an indication of the elasticity of Tibetan spirit types, certain *gyelpo* and *tsen* spirits are also sometimes called *nöjin*.

- *nyen*: These sky spirits live in the atmospheric realms and can also cause diseases or calamities if provoked or disturbed. The word for these spirits literally means "mighty" or "awesome," and they are often iconographically presented with dark complexions. *Nyen* also have astrological associations and encompass multiple subtypes, such as "sun *nyen*," "moon *nyen*," "star *nyen*," and "planetary *nyen*."[52] Samten Karmay claims that the word can be used as an adjective for other spirits or objects, such as "*lha gnyan* [*lhanyen*], the 'awesome lha', *klu gnyan* [*lunyen*], the 'awesome klu', *sa gnyan* [*sanyen*], the 'awesome locality', [and] *mtsho gnyan* [*tsonyen*], the 'awesome lake'."[53] However, like the astrological *nyen*, these likely refer to other subtypes or hybrid spirits and would be better translated as "celestial *nyen*," "serpent *nyen*," "earth *nyen*," and "lake *nyen*."

- *sadak*, *yülha*, *zhidak*: These spirits are local deities who are tied to a specific region, mountain, or valley. Often these deities must be propitiated whenever a building is going to be constructed or crops planted on the land that they inhabit. These spirits are the epitome of indigenous

---

[48] Nebesky-Wojkowitz 1998, p. 6; see also pp. 18, 24.

[49] For more on *mamo*, see Blondeau 2002.

[50] See Tucci 1999, vol. 2, pp. 713–717. For more on the first Tibetan clans and their mythic descent from a demoness, see Sørensen 1994, pp. 125–133.

[51] See Sutherland 1991.   [52] See Reb gong pa 2009, p. 79.

[53] Karmay 1998h, pp. 443.

Tibetan deities and a Tibetan's soul is believed to be under the dominion of the *sadak* of the land where they were born.[54]

- *si*: Like the *dre*, this term also refers to a broad category of malevolent spirits. They are often described as having human bodies with animal heads, such as a weasel, pig, or goat, depending on the subcategory of *si*. Confusingly, many si are also categorically associated with other spirit types because they are mythically said to reside in their lands, such as *gyelsi*, *tsensi*, or *lusi*. There are also *si* that specifically harm or eat children (*chungsi*), men (*posi*), and women (*mosi*). Perhaps the most famous kind of *si*, however, is the *damsi*, who are believed to have violated their religious vows in past lives and who can inspire individuals to do the same.[55]

- *sinpo*: These spirits are associated with the Indian demons called *rākṣasas*, the most common demons encountered in the Indian epics. While the indigenous imagery of the *lu* was glossed over by Indian iconography, these malevolent spirits bear little resemblance to their Indian counterparts other than enjoying eating human flesh. *Sinpo* are often depicted as black in complexion with wild, long, black hair and wearing animal-skin loin cloths.[56]

- *teurang*: These are ancient Tibetan spirits that are primarily associated with the sky. They are also harmful and cause death and disease, indicating the common anxieties and misfortunes that many Tibetan spirits engender. They are said to have one leg and ride tornadoes as mounts. Gamblers frequently propitiate *teurang* for success at cards or dice; however, if they receive the *teurangs'* blessings they will be reborn as their servants.[57] Erik Haarh explains that these deities were originally the spirits of pre-Buddhist ancestors found in the heavenly spheres.[58]

---

[54] See Schuh 2012 and Buffetrille 2002.

[55] See Nebesky-Wojkowitz 1998, pp. 300–303. In keeping with the habit of scholars using familiar western demonological terms to translate certain Tibetan spirits, Charles Ramble has taken to calling these beings vampires, based on their penchant for drinking blood; see, for example, Ramble 2015 and 2017.

[56] See Kelényi 2003, pp. 4, 31, and Farkas and Szabó 2002, pp. 61, 73.

[57] See Kornman et al. 2015, pp. 532 n. 66, 598.

[58] See Haarh 1969, pp. 216–219, and Berounský 2010.

- *tsen*: Like *gyelpo*, the name of these spirits also means "king" or "emperor," owing to the term originating during the imperial age. These indigenous Tibetan deities are known to be war-like and wrathful. They are usually red in color and are generally believed to be the spirits of past monks who have rejected their Buddhist vows. Todd Gibson explores this specific spirit type in his doctoral dissertation, arguing that they are a deification of the Tibetan imperial line.[59]

- *werma*: These warrior spirits are closely associated with *dralha* and are predominantly found in Bön classifications, as well as in the epic of Gesar. As such, they are protectors of Gesar and of warriors in general. According to one scheme, there are thirteen principal *werma*, each associated with a different animal, much like the *si*.[60]

- *ẓa*: These spirits personify the planets and are thus correlated with the Sanskrit *graha*. Many of these deities have been adopted from Indian astrology, the most popular of which is Rāhula.[61] Tibetan astrological calculations are an important precursor to most rituals, particularly those pertaining to site consecration, as well as to rites of passage such as birthing ceremonies and weddings. Planetary deities must therefore be propitiated and sometimes pacified on these occasions.

For all of these major spirit types, one can find examples of individuals with distinct personalities as well as more amorphous numbered groups – usually in odd numbers like five, nine, thirteen, or fifteen. Many of these kinds of representations will be further encountered in the sections that follow.

Spirit Ontologies

Delineating spirit types reveals significant nuances but should not elide the fact that the boundaries between them are porous. Geoffrey Samuel relates the Tibetan pantheon to the Tibetan political system with its historical lack of centralization and formal bureaucratic structure.[62] I agree in principle; however, I would add that the above typology of Tibetan spirits is more

---

[59] See Gibson 1991.
[60] See Snellgrove 1967, pp. 44–65, and Kornman et al. 2015, pp. xxxix.
[61] See Bailey 2012 and 2019a. [62] See Samuel 1993, p. 167.

akin to different Tibetan clans.[63] Each spirit type is a nonhuman clan with its own qualities and attributes, and there are many instances where they "intermarry." Some deities are even a combination of two classes. For instance, a spirit that is both a *ẓa* and a *dü*, having come from a father of one and a mother of the other, will be called a *ẓa dü*. The connection between clans and spirits is more overt with the *mönpa*, which refers to both an ethnic clan that inhabited southern Tibet and to spirits found within certain deity retinues.[64]

Beyond dizzying arrays of spirit typologies, these beings are further categorized within a heavily Buddhist ontological scheme involving four major divisions. First, there are the buddhas, bodhisattvas, and tutelary deities (*yidam*; Skt. *iṣṭadevatā*) of Tantric Buddhism. These enlightened beings are encountered at the highest levels of Buddhist monastic ritual practice and yogic meditation. Second, there are the supramundane protector deities (*jiktenledepé sungma*; Skt. *lokottara*), who are emanations of buddhas and bodhisattvas; such beings are not usually concerned with mundane worldly affairs. Third, there are the mundane protector deities (*jiktenpé sungma*; Skt. *laukika*), who are associated with geographical features and subject to the laws of karma. These deities are focused on worldly affairs and constantly interact with humans.[65] Fourth, there is the horde of unconverted local spirits and ghosts, who often bring illness, bad luck, and calamity. The middle two categories are taken up with Dharma protectors, which are propitiated to protect and maintain the Buddhist or Bön teachings. According to Samuel, the last two categories of mundane protectors and malevolent local spirits are not wholly distinct and there is a degree of fluidity between them.[66] This diffusion is because most mundane deities were once local spirits that were tamed and now serve the Buddhist teachings, a concept that will be examined later. For their part, local spirits are still considered pernicious and are often placed within the retinues of

---

[63] Tucci (1999, vol. 2, pp. 711–730) made a similar observation.

[64] The clan and spirit intersections of the *mönpa* are discussed in Nebesky-Wojkowitz 1998, pp. 8–11.

[65] For a fuller examination of the ontological nature of these latter two categories across the Indo-Tibetan Buddhist world, see Ruegg 2008.

[66] See Samuel 1993, pp. 166–167.

mundane deities. Fluidity exists across all four divisions and there is some mobility between them, since deities are thought to move up in classification over time as their karmic actions become more purified. Much of the disagreement between schools and lineages concerns the violent nature of these spirits, and whether their seemingly wrathful actions and interactions are legitimized through Mahāyana skillful means or karmic consequences.

Spirit taxonomies consistently lack uniformity and systematization, despite attempts over the centuries by numerous religious authorities to establish such consistency. This indicates that Tibetan spirit types, their traits, and their values are context specific and relative to the regional communities in which they are encountered. If religion is ultimately local then so are demonologies, as are the practices used to categorically, spatially, materially, and temporally delimit them. The remainder of this work will offer concrete examples that clarify the importance of these otherwise abstract concepts. Each section concerns a different thematic arena of distinct ritual and mythic significance in how Tibetans interact with numerous kinds of spirits. The first section, "Spirits and the Body," concerns voluntary and involuntary acts of spirit possession, with the former illustrated by human oracles and the later resulting in various illnesses and misfortunes in need of medicinal or talismanic remedies. The second section, "Spirits and Time," discusses the importance of Tibetan astrology as well as cultural and monastic ritual calendars, both of which concern when certain spirits should or might be encountered during various activities on a daily, monthly, and yearly basis. The third section, "Spirits and Space," explores sky, land, and subterranean spirits that fill the Tibetan cosmic landscape, with special attention given to the importance of mountain deities. The final section, "Spirits and Doctrine," focuses on the significance and characterization of Dharma protectors and the ritual specialists who are revered or called upon to hold them to their vows to guard religious teachings and institutions. This structure is necessarily limited, since Tibetan spirits could also be explored across numerous other axes, such as ecology, animals, ritual evolution, material culture, translocal orientations, and historical eras. Many of the studies cited in this work have done just that with greater attention to detail. In the service of brevity, however, I have chosen themes that resonate with both Tibetan emic conceptions of activity within space, time, the body, and institutional religions, and with arenas of violent activity in which demonological engagement takes place. For that reason, many of the spirit types or deities briefly encountered in one section may make appearances elsewhere in greater detail, illustrating how they exist in multiple thematic contexts and offer diverse opportunities for interaction. Given the capricious nature of Tibetan spirits, violent personalities and practices underlie all of these themes, either through harmful actions on their part, liturgical retaliations from ritualists, or the dispatching of such beings to harm others.

I Spirits and the Body

Voluntary Possession

In the Tibetan worldview, spirits can interact with the human body in two major ways: through either voluntary or involuntary possession. Voluntary possession concerns intentional oracular trances, though often with violent behaviors and outcomes, while involuntary possession refers to unwelcome spirits causing illnesses, soul loss, or bodily afflictions. A Tibetan oracle is a human being who periodically and ritually becomes possessed by a Tibetan protector deity in order to provide prophecies or advice on anything from personal matters of health and well-being to state matters of national security. There are a number of Tibetan words that refer to oracles, such as *kuten* ("bodily receptacle"), *lhabap* ("god descent"), and *lhaka* ("god speech"). These terms are descriptive enough, yet others exist with varying degrees of popular usage and cultural significance. *Pawo* and *pamo* – meaning male and female warrior, respectively – focus more on the aggressive qualities of these figures.[67] Hildegard Diemberger argues that these terms also tie oracles to the epic bard traditions of Tibet and draw attention to the dangerous experiences that are commonly found in the life narratives of oracles.[68] Nebesky-Wojkowitz makes a distinction between terms used for oracles that channel low-ranking deities, such as *lhapa* ("god person"), and those used for high-ranking, state-recognized oracles, like

---

[67] Per-Arne Berglie (1976) frequently encounters this term in her fieldwork.

[68] See Diemberger 2005, p. 128; see also Stein 1959.

chöjé ("Dharma lord").[69] A term one also frequently encounters is *chökyong* (Skt. *dharmapāla*; "Dharma protector"),[70] which is confusing since it is more commonly applied to the deities themselves. Equally confusing is the use of *kandroma* to refer to female oracles in some instances,[71] which speaks to the polysemous nature of this and many of the other terms we encounter. In practice, *chökyong* is used to refer to the oracle while under possession by the deity, while other terms, such as *kuten* and *koktu ẓhukpa* ("the one who entered the torso"), refer to the medium who becomes possessed.[72]

The origins of the oracle tradition are unknown, though it is generally accepted to have been a pre-Buddhist practice that was later incorporated into Buddhist and Bön institutional and cosmological structures.[73] Generally, only worldly deities are believed to possess mediums, since transcendental deities are beyond the worldly concerns that oracles are requested to resolve. Rare instances where oracles claim to be possessed by transcendental deities are usually met with suspicion.[74] A medium is commonly renowned for being the vessel of a specific deity; however, most mediums can channel multiple deities in a single oracular trance, with each deity providing further insight into a communal crisis or prophetic declaration.[75]

---

[69] See Nebesky-Wojkowitz 1998, p. 409.

[70] Personal correspondence with a lama of Tengyeling monastery, Lhasa, July 2005. See also Tewari 1987, p. 140.

[71] See Diemberger 2005, p. 147. [72] See Nair 2004, p. 38 n. 8.

[73] See Nebesky-Wojkowitz 1998, p. 428, Peter 1978b, p. 288, and Tewari 1987.

[74] See Nebesky-Wojkowitz 1998, p. 409, and Diemberger 2005, p. 130. There are instances where enlightened beings are believed to possess and deliver prophesies through the medium of sacred objects. At Tradruk Temple (*Khra 'brug*), southeast of Lhasa, for example, there is a statue of Padmasambhava that supposedly has the ability to speak; see Dowman 1988, p. 178. For a complete monograph of Traduk, see Sørensen et al. 2005. There is a speaking image of Tārā (*Gsung sgrol ma*) at Langtang Drolma Temple (*Glang thang sgrol ma lha khang*) in Kham, west of Derge (*Sde dge*); see Dorje 2004, pp. 510–511. There is also a talking painting of Penden Lhamo in the Potala Palace; see Pommaret 2003b, p. 98.

[75] See Havnevik 2002, pp. 276–277, and Nebesky-Wojkowitz 1998, p. 421. For a detailed account of a single trance that involved four deities, see Ibid, pp. 433–437.

When a deity descends into a medium it results in a trance state, which evinces a marked change in the behavior of the medium. As the deity begins to possess the medium's body, he or she will begin to shake and tremble, breathe faster and heavier, and even puff out air or wag their tongue. The medium's complexion also changes, with their face turning red or yellow, depending on the disposition of the deity.[76] This disposition is important, since a medium can channel a wrathful or peaceful deity. A medium possessed by a wrathful deity will grow red-faced and become very violent in his or her movements; a passive deity will cause a medium to act more subdued. It is generally held that mediums of wrathful deities do not live very long because of the intense strain and pain they endure during trances.[77] The medium will also start to exhibit the specific attributes of the particular deity possessing them. Nebesky-Wojkowitz provides a vivid account of this feature:

> Many mediums, mostly at the beginning of the trance, show also a behaviour characteristic of the deity who took possession of their body. Thus a medium of *rDo rje shugs ldan* [Dorjé Shukden] produces the gurgling sound of a man in the agony of suffocation – said to be the voice of the abbot *bSod nams grags pa* [Sönam Drakpa] who killed himself by stuffing a ceremonial scarf into his throat –; the oracle-priest of *sKar ma shar* [Karmashar], who sometimes becomes possessed by *Bya khri mig gcig po* [Jatri Mikchikpo], "the one-eyed with the bird-throne", will keep only one eye open for the duration of his trance; the spirit of *Slob dpon* [Lopön], the crippled adversary of the former state magician [Nechung Oracle] *rGyal mtshan mthar phyin* [Gyentsen Tarchin], makes his medium limp; the *Drung yig chen mo* [Drungyik Chenmo], as soon as he had entered the body of an oracle-priest, will

---

[76] This process has been well documented: see Nebesky-Wojkowitz 1998, pp. 418–419, 429–431; Havnevik 2002, pp. 271–272; Day 1989, pp. 435–476; Day 1990, pp. 213–218; Berglie 1976, pp. 99–103; Schenk 1993; Diemberger 2005, pp. 136–138; and Makley 2018, pp. 95–96.

[77] See Nebesky-Wojkowitz 1998, pp. 418, 435, and Havnevik 2002, p. 272.

remind all those present of the events which led eventually to
his incorporation among the *dharmapālas* by saying the sen-
tence "I killed the ninety-nine horses of my master but left
one for my lady-love"; the spirit of the *las dpon* [foreman],
who once served the *bDe legs rabs ldan* [Delek Rapden] family
of Shigatse, always complains about the heavy grain-tax
which had been collected at his time, etc.[78]

Hanna Havnevik likewise describes a scenario in which the female oracle
Lobsang Tsedrön channeled a male warrior spirit and accordingly dressed,
walked, and drank beer "like a man"; she never drank beer in any other
circumstance. Patrons claim that, once out of the trance, nobody could smell
beer on her breath.[79]

Nonhuman qualities are a significant attribute of the trance state and help
authenticate the sacred activity that surrounds the oracle tradition. These
abilities include shows of super strength, such as being able to bear the
heavy crown associated with the position of the oracle, which is said to be so
heavy that two or three men are needed to hoist it onto the oracle's head.
Oracles have also been known to twist swords into knots, called "knotted
thunderbolts" (*dorjé düpa*), which are considered prized possessions among
Tibetans; those honored enough to obtain one hang it above doorways to
ward off demonic influences. Other feats of nonhuman ability gained under
trance include an oracle thrusting a sword into his or her chest and
removing it to show no sign of injury, and oracles vomiting coins.[80] Such
miraculous exhibitions accompany the oracle's primary skills of clairvoyance and prophecy that are the impetus for their trances.[81]

Oracle trances serve the community on multiple levels. This service
involves eliciting the nonhuman knowledge of the deity as expressed
through the oracle to provide prophetic advice concerning the future of
the community. With village oracles the concern is more local, while state

---

[78] Nebesky-Wojkowitz 1998, p. 418.   [79] See Havnevik 2002, p. 271.

[80] See Rock 1935, p. 477, and Nebesky-Wojkowitz 1998, pp. 440–441.

[81] For a detailed examination of the Buddhist understanding of clairvoyance, see
Nair 2010, p. 26 n. 27.

oracles such as Nechung offer advice on a greater political scale. An oracle can be consulted by individual patrons regarding personal crises, such as family problems or wealth and love issues, or for communal concerns, such as unsolved crimes and legal matters.[82] On the local level oracles can act as healers, using their powers of divination to assess an individual's illness and respond with appropriate advice as to its remedy. Nebesky-Wojkowitz describes a ritual called "releasing the obstructing spirit" (*gekdröl*), where an oracle will beat a sick individual with their sword in order to drive away the harmful forces causing the illness.[83]

The life narratives of oracles often have similar patterns. Diemberger explains that the life story usually involves the future medium first experiencing chronic physical and/or mental illness, such as "uncontrolled visions, voices, fainting, weakness, and the experience of a death-like state."[84] After consulting a lama or oracle, the person's illness may be attributed to a divinity attempting to reside in their subtle body channels, which will need to be opened and purified. If the "god sickness" (*lhané*) is successfully remedied, the medium will be recognized as such and their possessions will be ritually voluntary and consistent. Diemberger claims that on a social scale the crisis that triggers the "god sickness" and subsequent initiation into oracular practice likely reflects personal difficulties with social constraints, especially in the case of female oracles, who often grapple with the restrictive expectations placed upon women in their communities.[85] Given such difficult experiences, the success of an oracle is likewise related to his or her ability to mediate at times of personal and public crisis. An oracle's reputation is dependent on their efficacy, so that a good track record of reliable predictions and ritual therapies will increase their prestige, while failed cures and claims will reduce it.[86] There are many accounts of oracles who have tarnished their reputation by offering bad or incorrect advice. On a political level, this can be especially hazardous. Nebesky-Wojkowitz relays an incident where the Nechung Oracle in 1904 predicted a Tibetan victory against the British

---

[82] See Diemberger 2005, pp. 115–116, 139, and Havnevik 2002, p. 271.

[83] See Nebesky-Wojkowitz 1998, p. 441. [84] Diemberger 2005, p. 120.

[85] See Ibid, pp. 119–120, 128–130. [86] See Ibid, pp. 138–140.

Expeditionary Force. This clearly did not occur, so the oracle fled with the Dalai Lama to Mongolia when the British reached Lhasa. Upon their return, the Nechung Oracle was dismissed from his office.[87] The punishment incurred by oracles for their inadequacy or insubordination has been known to come from the possessing deity as well. Such wrath is usually retaliation for the medium's disobedience to the deity. In one instance, recounted by Joseph Rock, a medium of Dorjé Shukden was requested by the deity not to marry, yet did so anyway. In response, during a fit of trance the deity caused the medium to disembowel himself and hang his entrails on the statues in his private chapel.[88]

It is never quite clear why a particular individual is chosen to be an oracle. Mediums can appear among the monastic or lay community; for instance, the Nechung mediums have mostly been monks,[89] while the Gadong medium has always been a layman and the lineage was hereditary.[90] In most cases, an individual is chosen by a deity for their own mysterious reasons, though Tibetans speculate that there is a moral element to this choice. Some claim that an oracle must live a blameless and virtuous life in order to be a vessel pure enough for a deity to inhabit temporarily.[91] However, it is also claimed that mediums tend to be of low moral quality. This may be specific only to local mediums, where a distinction is drawn between the aristocratic and lower-class laity – the latter being from where mediums generally come.[92] Diemberger argues that mediums have a comfortable relationship with defilement, having experienced it in their own lives and having dealt with it in healing practices. This familiarity gives mediums a degree of insight afforded by their ambiguous social status. Ambiguity allows mediums to resolve personal and public crises that generally develop from liminal moments of life such as birth, marriage, sickness, and death, all of which

---

[87] See Nebesky-Wojkowitz 1998, p. 451.

[88] See Rock 1935, p. 478. Nebesky-Wojkowitz (1998, p. 421) also cites this example.

[89] According to the Gadong Medium of the 1990s, the Nechung mediumship started out as lay, but this lineage broke early and became monastic instead; see Kelley 1993, p. 20.

[90] See Ibid, p. 29. Havnevik 2002 explicitly examines a hereditary oracle lineage.

[91] See Rock 1935, p. 478, and Nebesky-Wojkowitz 1998, p. 418.

[92] See Havnevik 2002, p. 277, and Day 1990, p. 208.

are fraught with impurities.[93] Nonetheless, mediums are expected to maintain a degree of bodily purity by abstaining from tobacco and alcohol, and by following any prohibitions requested by the possessing deity.[94] Regarding medium recognition on a political level, there are some instances in which a potential medium is chosen from a series of candidates, with various tests administered to aid the selection process. Nebesky-Wojkowitz details this process and explains that a successful candidate is installed in his position during a ceremony called *tendrel* ("auspicious circumstance"), which involves gift giving and the conferring of titles on the newly appointed medium.[95]

Nebesky-Wojkowitz attended a number of trance sessions firsthand and his account of oracle possession, though sixty years old, continues to be the most descriptive and organized in its presentation.[96] The ceremony involves a lot of preparation. The special attire worn by the medium during a trance is laid out on a throne or seat in the specific order in which the medium dresses. The clothes in this ensemble are indicative of the possessing deity and include various weapons associated with them. Another important item that oracles – especially state oracles – wear is a small shield with a *mantric* seed syllable inscribed on it, which hangs around the neck and rests upon the medium's chest. Seed syllables are single syllables of great power and many deities of all ontological statuses are associated with a particular one. This oracular shield is actually a mirror (*melong*), since it is reflective and convex at the center, and sometimes has a gold or silver rim.

Once the preparations are complete, the monks attending the trance session begin a series of invocatory chants inviting the deity to come and possess the medium. This invocation can include musical accompaniment from thigh-bone trumpets and drums. Havnevik provides an example in which the oracle herself chants the invocations and thus prompts the deity to descend of her own accord without the aid of monks. This stage of the ceremony also includes detailed iconographic descriptions of the deity as

[93] See Diemberger 2005, pp. 141–150. [94] See Havnevik 2002, p. 280 n. 115.
[95] See Nebesky-Wojkowitz 1998, pp. 419–421. See also Bell 2013, pp. 209–214.
[96] For a more recent anthropological account of the Nechung Oracle's trance state, observed in Dharamsala, see Sidky 2011. See also Danzang Cairang 2009 and Makley 2018, pp. 67–104.

well as the deity's abode. As the chanting continues, the deity is said to descend gradually upon the oracle, forcing him or her to fall deeper into a trance state. This transition is punctuated by huffing breath and violent movements that grow steadily exaggerated. For the Nechung Oracle, the face assumes a dark red color and his assistants place the heavy helmet upon his head, fastening it with belts under his chin. Assistants are usually available during the entire ceremony to help dress the oracle, hold them up, and catch them when they collapse at the end of the trance. Havnevik explains that for the female state oracle Lobsang Tsedrön, her husband was her assistant during trances.[97] When the assistants step back and the oracle bears the helmet alone, the deity is believed to have fully descended. At this point of the trance praise is sung to the oracle, the deity embodied, and he or she is ready to attend to the needs of those present. Tea and sometimes ritual dough cakes (*torma*) are offered to the oracle. If the ceremony takes place within the actual throne room of the deity, then the oracle sits on their own throne. If the ceremony takes place within the home of a client, the deity is treated like an honored guest. Even retired oracles continue to be revered by monks and patrons.

Once praise has been offered, the oracle is asked various questions by the surrounding monks or present members of the community. The answers to these questions are in most instances quite cryptic and require translation by the assistants, showing a further act of mediation. The trance session is an engaged process; the esoteric and mumbled advice of the oracle is clarified by the interpreting assistants and then enacted by the individual or members of the community. In effect, the oracle is only one element – though an important one – in a complex system of communal decision-making. Answers can also be provided in verse. In some instances, the trance is framed by moments of wild frenzied dancing performed by the oracle (Fig. 1), as well as the various shows of superhuman ability previously described.

After all questions have been answered, the oracle may provide an extra service of offering blessings, either by blowing on barley seeds or inscribing prayers on tied ribbons, both of which are then given to members of the audience. The service ends abruptly when the oracle collapses. The deity

---

[97] See Havnevik 2002, p. 274.

Figure 1 The Nechung Oracle dancing in a state of possession; Nechung Monastery, Dharamsala 2016 (photo: Cecilia Haynes)

departs, the human faculties of the medium return, and sometimes he or she passes out; the medium has no recollection of the proceedings of the session. Several trance sessions may occur during one ceremony, with each trance signifying the descent of another spirit into the medium. Usually the first to enter is the central god with whom the oracle is most associated. This god is called the "lord of the channels" (*tsadak*) and is the one who allows other deities to enter the medium. At the conclusion of the ceremony, prayers of thanksgiving are often recited. The medium then strips off the oracular attire and replaces it in proper order on the throne with the help of his or her assistants. Usually the normal garments of the medium, which are worn beneath this attire, are drenched in sweat after a ceremony.[98]

This summary of an oracle trance ceremony is by necessity both generic and synchronic. Multiple variations of the ceremony exist at various points in Tibetan history and differ by locale. One important note should be made on the diachronic nature of the sources cited here. Nebesky-Wojkowitz, writing in the 1950s, provides a detailed examination of the oracle tradition as it existed in the midst of Chinese occupation but before the Cultural Revolution. His focus is also strongly directed toward important male state oracles. This observation is the same for Joseph Rock and Prince Peter of Greece and Denmark, both of whom conducted preliminary research on the oracle tradition as it existed before or just after Chinese occupation. Hanna Havnevik, Hildegard Diemberger, and Charlene Makley, however, conducted their research well after the Cultural Revolution, a time when the practices of many oracle lineages were forcefully cut off. This also resulted in the destruction of many oracle costumes and ritual implements. In these studies, the majority of oracles do not change into ceremonial garments and their only ritual implement consists of a mirror that they use for divination purposes. Havnevik, Diemberger, and Makley, as well as Sophie Day, provide useful studies on the state of the oracle tradition as it exists in recent times, and all of their studies show an increase in members of the tradition, mainly in villages and on the local level. Diemberger's work further emphasizes how some female oracles not only engage in collective politics of ethnic resistance, but even ally themselves with the ruling Communist party.[99] Nevertheless, since the Fourteenth Dalai Lama escaped to India in 1959, state-recognized oracles no longer exist in Tibet; even the one female state oracle, Lobsang Tsedrön, retired.

---

[98] For the full accounts of oracle trances from which this summary draws, see Nebesky-Wojkowitz 1998, pp. 409–439; Havnevik 2002, pp. 270–272; and Diemberger 2005, pp. 136–138.

[99] See Diemberger 2005, pp. 162–168.

Involuntary Possession

As violent as oracular possession often is, it contrasts sharply with the involuntary possession of harmful spirits believed to be the cause of misfortune, sickness, and even death. As Sienna Craig explains, misfortune and illness tap into a complex system of interrelating factors, such as karmic consequences, spiritual pollution, and personal misdeeds, as well as the harmful influences of various spirits and local gods.[100] Martin Mills makes a similar observation, condensing the intersecting influences of this socio-cosmic system into the following list:

- systems of bodily humours, and their various interrelationships;
- levels of *sparkha*, or life-force;
- demonological and pollution accounts; and
- matters of karmic retribution.[101]

Spirits may not be the only cause of misfortune or ailments, but they are a major one, so elaborate diagnostic methods have been developed in the Tibetan medical tradition in order to ascertain whether a malady is indeed the result of a spirit, and, if so, what kind.

The *Four Tantras*, mythically attributed to the Medicine Buddha Bhaiṣajyaguru and rediscovered in the twelfth century, are generally considered the foundational textual corpus of Tibetan medicine. In its exceedingly thorough discussion of medical practices, chapters 77 to 81 of the third tantra detail those illnesses and forms of madness thought to be caused by various evil spirits. These chapters use the spirit type *dön* in a much more generic fashion to mean any malicious or illness-causing spirit. Chapter 77 even offers its own demonology of eighteen such *dön*, classifying many of the spirits listed in the Introduction beneath this broader label. These 18 *dön* are: (1) *lha* (*deva*), (2) *lhamin* (*asura*), (3) *driza* (*gandharva*), (4) *lu* (*nāga*), (5) *nöjin* (*yakṣa*), (6) *tsangpa* (*Brahmā*), (7) *sinpo* (*rākṣasa*), (8) *shaza* (*piśāca*), (9) *yidak* (*preta*), (10) *trülbum*

---

[100] See Craig 2012, pp. 6, 128–129. I am grateful to William McGrath for drawing my attention to this work.

[101] Mills 2003, p. 244. For a fuller exploration of the relationship between pollution and karma, see Ibid, pp. 206–232.

(*kumbhāṇḍa*), (11) *jetem*,[102] (12) *yengjé* (*kiṭi*), (13) *rolang* (*vetāla*), (14) *tsünlha* (*kavya*), (15) *lama* (*guru*), (16) *drangsong* (*ṛṣi*), (17) *gen* (*vṛddha*), and (18) *drupa* (*siddha*).[103] I include the equivalent Sanskrit terms in parenthesis to highlight the heavily Indic Buddhist emphasis of the work. Intriguingly, this list is copied verbatim into a twentieth-century Bön medical text.[104] Nevertheless, the chapter on *dön* continues by elaborating on the various personality traits and behavioral changes someone can exhibit to indicate the spirit possessing them:

> [Those possessed by] a *lha* spirit will speak Sanskrit, use pleasant words, sleep little, have a noble countenance, and keep very clean. [Those possessed by] a *lhamin* will revere meat and liquor, look angrily out of the corner of their eyes, and be wrathful, full of pride, and very impetuous. [Those possessed by] a *driza* will be charming, sweet-smelling, and content with themselves. They will take pleasure in song, dance, and entertainment and crave red jewelry. [Those possessed by] a *lu* will have a radiant complexion, stare with piercing red eyes, crave white and red [offerings], have a wandering tongue, and sleep face down. [Those possessed by] a *nöjin* will delight in treasure and utter secrets. They will be averse to physicians and Brahmins and crave fish. [Those possessed by] a *tsangpa* will cry out "Kye!" and recite *śāstras*. They will strike themselves, revile others, and be fond of laughter. [Those possessed by] a *sinpo* will be strong, speak crude verses, and value red [offerings]. [Those possessed by] a *shaza* will feel ashamed, speak in a low voice, and sometimes have seizures. They will weep without reason,

---

[102] Referring to spirits created by curses, this is the only word in this list without an explicit Indian parallel.

[103] See Yon tan mgon po 1982, p. 385. I am grateful to Bryan Cuevas for introducing me to this chapter of the text.

[104] See Namkhai Norbu 1995, p. 142.

claw at the ground, and speak in a disjointed manner. [Those possessed by] a *yidak* will act in the manner of a *yidak*. [Those possessed by] a *miamchi* will tremble in fear and not desire food. [Those possessed by] a *trülbum* will have an angry countenance, move slowly, and have swollen testicles. [Those possessed by] a *jetem* will run naked while brandishing a stick and dwell in desolate places. They will wander, pant in thirst, burn with rage, and not desire food. [Those possessed by] a *rolang* will speak the truth, sleep deeply, delight in jewelry, and tremble. [Those possessed by] a *tsünlha* will have a dry mouth and squinting eyes and will put clothes on their left side [first]. [Those possessed by] the four – *lama*, *drang-song* (sages), *genpo* (elders), and *drupa* (realized ones) – will conduct themselves as, and [eat] the food corresponding to, each one. They will keep company with any young boy and strip naked. They will tuck up their hair and renounce unhealthy thoughts for a long time. The cure is to recite mantras, bestow burnt *torma* offerings, recite [religious texts], practice meditation, and accumulate merit. Through this, the evil spirits will be pacified.[105]

This lengthy portion ends with popular remedies for these afflictions, which involve several kinds of religious activities.

The most famous commentary on the *Four Tantras*, and a highly revered medical treatise in its own right, is the seventeenth-century *Blue Beryl* by Sangyé Gyatso (1653–1705), the final regent of the Fifth Dalai Lama (1617–1682). Sangyé Gyatso's examination of chapter 77 elaborates on these eighteen spirit types in relation to the maladies and personality changes they engender, and he describes each of them in greater detail.[106]

[105] Yon tan mgon po 1982, pp. 385–386.

[106] See Sangs rgyas rgya mtsho 1973, pp. 52–58. For more on these important texts and the Tibetan medical tradition in general, see Parfionovitch et al. 1992, and Gyatso 2015.

For instance, while the above description of someone possessed by a *yidak* spirit is quite terse, Sangyé Gyatso further describes them as having thin limbs on an emaciated body and yearning for food and drink. The spirits that take on the form of elders, called *gen(po)*, are further described as a type of *lha* spirit. They arrogantly presume they are the lords of all sentient beings because of their learning.[107] Moreover, Sangyé Gyatso commissioned elaborate medical paintings to accompany his masterpiece in the late seventeenth century. These paintings have since been copied several times over, including contemporary renditions that carefully reproduce every nuance of the originals.[108] The forty-sixth painting in particular provides images of the eighteen *dön* spirits described in chapter 77 of the *Four Tantras*, giving us greater insight into the iconography of these beings. For instance, the *driza* is shown with a horse's head on a human body and playing a Tibetan lute, referencing their *gandharva* roots as horse-headed celestial musicians. The *lu* is likewise illustrated in the more common Indic fashion with a human head, arms, and torso over a snake's tail for a bottom half. The *tsangpa* spirit, in turn, has four heads, indicating the close connection to Brahmā despite the plurality of this spirit type in this context.[109]

Beyond skillfully observing an afflicted individual, experienced physicians could also diagnosis spirit trauma through sphygmology, or reading one's pulse. In his study of such practices within a Tibetan medical text that is potentially older than the *Four Tantras*, William McGrath translates several chapter segments from the *Medicine of the Moon King* describing the subtle differences in a client's pulse. In chapter 23 of this text, entitled "Demonic Pulsations," the blood vessels of the radial artery at the wrist are felt for certain signs:

> If the Lung and Heart vessels quiver and halt, the affliction
> derives from non-Buddhist extremists disturbing gods and

---

[107] See Sangs rgyas rgya mtsho 1973, pp. 56–57.

[108] See Williamson and Young 2009.

[109] See Ibid, pp. 130–133, and Parfionovitch et al. 1992, pp. 263–264.

spirits [*lhandre*], fornicating in the woods or near a spring, in either a southern or western direction. If the Heart and Lung vessels swell, the affliction derives from bewitching or king spirits [*gyelgong*]. If the pulsations of the Lung and Heart vessels are taut, the affliction derives from a schoolmaster or abbot. If they are empty and floating, the affliction derives from graveyard spirits [*durtrö dre*]. If they are submerged and unclear, the affliction derives from household spirits [*kangpé dre*]. If they fluctuate, the affliction derives from farmland spirits [*zhing sadak*].[110]

Here the more common *dre* is used as a generic reference for malevolent spirits, rather than *dön* as above. Regardless, clearly there is an exacting medical practice when determining the demonic causes of ailments and afflictions under which one can fall.[111]

Once a spirit has been ascertained as the cause for involuntary possession or illness, there are numerous methods Tibetans can use to expel them. While religious activity is a popular recommendation, the most common way to contend with unwanted possession or the affliction of harmful spirits is through exorcistic rites. There are many implements and practices used for such rites, including magical diagrams and charms, sacred dances (*'chams*), and ransom offerings. Some of the most common charms commissioned by devotees from lamas and other advanced ritual specialists are *cakras* and *liṅgas*. *Cakras* are circular geometric patterns often containing protective mantras that ward off harmful spirits. *Liṅgas*, by contrast, are anthropomorphic illustrations of spirits and even human enemies, often shown bound with chains and assaulted by scorpions. Samten Karmay offers numerous examples of these ritual charms in his exploration of the Fifth Dalai Lama's secret autobiography and accompanying illustrations.[112]

---

[110] McGrath 2017, p. 508; translation by McGrath.

[111] For more on the connection between spirits and illness in Tibet, see Samuel 2007 and 2010, and Deane 2014, pp. 123–142.

[112] For examples of *liṅga*, including those that protect against *damsi*, illness-causing *dön*, and maleficent female spirits called *senmo*, see Karmay 1988, pp. 120–121,

In both cases, recitations accompanying the construction and execution of these paper effigies are believed to guard against particular spirits and enemies once they are empowered.

For sacred dances, which are generally performed at monasteries and other sacred sites by a monastic troupe, the ceremony often reaches a crescendo whereby an effigy of a demonic spirit is stabbed by the central exorcistic dancer or shot with an arrow. In this context, the spirit afflicts the body politic at large – the community as a whole – and needs to be exorcized and purified through ritual violence. The effigy of the spirit is either made of barley dough or drawn on a sheet paper, and is also sometimes burned as part of the ritual. In either case, the effigy is stabbed by a ritual dagger (*purbu*) and the spirit is thought to be benevolently slain in order to secure for them an auspicious rebirth, as well as to neutralize the threat they pose to the local community and to religious harmony overall. The compassionate killing of sentient beings, even malicious ones, is not accepted without troubled reflection or shaky theological justifications, a matter Richard Kohn observes in his ethnographic observations of the Mani Rimdu ritual dance performed by Tibetan monastic communities in Nepal.[113]

On a smaller scale, if a family member is struggling with a spirit illness, village oracles can be entreated for their services as exorcistic healers. Once the spirit type causing an illness has been uncovered through divination or by reading symptoms, a medicinal and religious course of action is generally recommended. Often the family is asked by the oracle to commission certain rites, pay for the renovation of a reliquary, or make various offerings at a monastery or temple. The entranced oracle will also sometimes use their mouth to suck out the "polluting" (*drip*) influence.[114] For a family of means,

138–139, 144–145, 154–155, 162, and 165–169. For examples of *cakras*, including those that ward off spirits like *gongpo*, *damsi*, *senmo*, *söndre*, and *shidre*, see Karmay 1988, pp. 69, 170–173. For an exploration of the history of *liṅga* effigy iconography, see Cuevas 2011. See also Waddell 1973, pp. 115–128. For more on the soteriological range of amulets, see Gentry 2017, pp. 236–259.

[113] See Kohn 2001, pp. 73–86. For more on Tibetan sacred dances, see Nebesky-Wojkowitz 1976 and Samuel 2017.

[114] See Diemberger 2005, pp. 122, 138, 157.

when one of their members is especially ill it is not uncommon for them to consult both oracles and monastic specialists for assistance.

When lamas and monks are commissioned to perform cleansing rituals, they will be hired for a fee to construct a ransom offering (*lütor*) to dispel malevolent spirits. It is often believed that after a death in the family the negative forces that caused it will linger over the home and create further disturbances and misfortunes. If such signs are evident and persist, monks will visit the house to prepare the ransom through their ritual ministrations. The ritual object constructed by the monks usually consists of a barley dough effigy (representing the victim) placed in a box with other smaller dough offerings and topped with a multicolored thread cross. Family members can also help make the smaller dough offerings by hand. The belief is that the spirit will be drawn to these offerings and the effigy, confusing it for the afflicted person, and then become trapped in the thread cross. By some accounts the thread cross is thought to be a beautiful palace that attracts the spirit, who willingly resides in it. In either instance, the power of the ritual objects is imbued through mantras and liturgical texts recited by the monks as they construct them. Traditionally, once the exorcistic object was completed, it was to be carried to a crossroads or the edge of the village and left to either be scavenged by wild animals or lit and burnt. In both instances the evil influence was believed to then scatter to the four directions. This ritual continues to be performed in Tibet today; however, it has been modernized to a degree in order to accommodate the realities of contemporary city life. In Lhasa, for instance, it is the general practice for a young and healthy family member to carry the ransom offering off to a street crossroads where cars can run it over. The family member would be blessed by one of the hired monks beforehand with a prayer scarf placed over their shoulders. Once they have dispatched the offering, the family member must return home without talking to anyone or looking back at the object for fear that the spirit will follow them and return to the household.[115] When not actively avoiding them, cars or buses will run over the offering in the middle of the street and destroy the harmful influence.

---

[115] Personal correspondence, Tibetan interviewee, July 25, 2005. See also Barnett 2012.

These ransom rituals have been in practice for at least a millennium, since such texts have been found at Dunhuang.[116] Popular ritual texts recited during the construction process today include the *Wish-fulfilling Tree that Benefits All and the Bliss Practiced in the Royal Palace: A Ransom Offering Ritual*[117] by the Third Tukwan Lozang Chökyi Nyima (1737–1802), a famous Geluk master, and the *Supplication Clearing the Path of Obstacles*,[118] a treasure text revealed by the Nyingma and nonsectarian figure Chokgyur Lingpa (1829–1870).[119] Whether it involves an effigy of the spirit to be destroyed, expelled, or imprisoned, medicinal and oracular healing, or ransom offerings, these diverse exorcism rites provide a common method for resolving involuntary possession and misfortune brought about by malevolent spirits.

II Spirits and Time

Tibetans encounter spirits throughout the traditional lunar year. Astrological consequences are tied to spirit interactions, the movements of the planets are identified with powerful and often demonic beings, and Tibetan festivals or the ritual calendars of monasteries engage with various divinities and spirits on a monthly basis. Tibetans subscribe to a rich system of astrology, portions of which were inherited from and influenced by both India and China for more than a millennium. This system ascribes divine identities to the planets, constellations, and celestial bodies – with the most

---

[116] See cataloged texts IOL Tib J 420 and IOL TIB J 569 of the International Dunhuang Project (http://idp.bl.uk/) for examples.

[117] The Tibetan title is *glud gtor gyi cho ga kun phan 'dod 'jo dang / rgyal rdzong lag tu blang bde ba*; see Blo bzang chos kyi nyi ma 1969–1971. These and numerous other Tibetan texts can be viewed online at the Buddhist Digital Resource Center (www.tbrc.org/).

[118] The Tibetan title is *gsol 'debs bar chad lam sel*; see Mchog gyur gling pa 1976.

[119] For the most extensive treatment of this ritual, with a focus on modern iterations, see Barnett 2012. See also Beyer 1978, pp. 310–359; Karmay 1998c and 1998d; Nebesky-Wojkowitz and Gorer 1950–1951; and Nebesky-Wojkowitz 1998, pp. 343–397.

famous planetary spirit being Rāhula – and these forces help govern the fates of individuals. Astrology also provides opportunities to overpower spirits or respond to their activities.

An astrological chart (*sipaho*) is often found in Tibetan homes. This chart not only illustrates the twelve zodiac animals of the years and diagrammatic representations of the eight trigrams (*parka degyé*) – both drawn from Chinese astrology, hemerology, and divination – but it is also used as an amulet to draw auspiciousness to the household and ward off evil spirits. The eight trigrams themselves are anthropomorphized as *sadak* spirits, and the Fifth Dalai Lama classifies the astrological deities in general as *sadak*.[120] Since these are predominantly land spirits, this intimately ties Tibetan astrology to the landscape as well.[121] For instance, when houses are built or wells dug, *sadak* must be properly propitiated on certain favorable days in order to secure their permission before "injuring" the land. *Nyen* must also be properly attended to by not cutting down the trees they are believed to inhabit for timber, except on certain days recommended by an almanac.[122] Along with karmic consequences, such spirit-based calamities are really a matter of being in the wrong place at the wrong time. As noted earlier, these spirits and their iconography are drawn from both Buddhist and indigenous influences; however, many of the *sadak* have Chinese origins as well, given its strong impact on Tibetan astrology.[123]

Like the foundational medical text of the *Blue Beryl*, the Fifth Dalai Lama's regent Sangyé Gyatso authored an equally seminal work on Tibetan astrology and calendrics entitled the *White Beryl*. The *sadak*, and other spirits of the land such as the female *men*, are described extensively in this work.[124] In keeping with the locative as well as temporal character of these spirits, the *sadak* are believed to inhabit the quarters of the cardinal and

---

[120] See Kelényi 2003, pp. 49–50, and Tucci 1999, vol. 2, pp. 722–724.

[121] See Cornu 2002, pp. 245–246. See also Kelényi 2012.

[122] See Cornu 2002, p. 248. [123] See Tucci 1999, vol. 2, p. 723.

[124] Nebesky-Wojkowitz (1998, pp. 291–298) provides a partial but informative list of the most frequently mentioned *sadak* in the text. For the original Tibetan chapter, see Sangs rgyas rgya mtsho 1972, pp. 255–334. This text also offers vivid illustrations of the numerous *sadak* spirits.

ordinal directions, as well as various other realms of the world.[125] The king of the *sadak* travels from year to year, occupying the directional realms associated with the animal of each year. As Philippe Cornu explains, "in the Year of the Rat, he is in the North, in the Year of the Cow he is in the Northeast, and so on."[126] The king's consorts and retinue likewise move with the years.

Beyond the spirits of the earth, Tibetan tradition recognizes eight planets that correspond to certain divinities. Béla Kelényi describes these "Eight Great Planets" (*ʒachen gyé*), along with the symbols that represent them in astrological diagrams and charts:

> [there are] the Sun (disk), regarded as a planet, and the Moon (crescent), and the five visible planets known in ancient times: Mars (eye), Mercury (hand), Jupiter (ritual dagger), Venus (arrowhead), Saturn (fibre-bundle); in addition to these, Rahu[la] and Ketu (bird head) [counted as one], symbolising the points where the ascending and descending orbit of the Moon intersects the ecliptic plane.[127]

Rāhula, Chief of the Planetary Gods

We turn now to Rāhula, given his particular importance as the chief of the *ʒa* spirits and thus most often encountered in related Tibetan rites and practices. Rāhula stems from Indian astrology and, along with Ketu (cited above), he signifies not one of the known planets but more so the ascending node of the moon that results in eclipses. With Ketu indicating the descending node of the moon, the two beings are often treated as one giant being who swallows the sun or the moon, causing an eclipse. In their earlier Hindu incarnation, when the two beings are treated separately, Rāhula is a disembodied head while Ketu is the decapitated body. When Rāhula devours the sun or moon, it eventually exits from his neck.[128]

In his extensive exploration of Rāhula's mythos and significance, Cameron Bailey examines the deity's Hindu and Indian Buddhist origins

---

[125] See Nebesky-Wojkowitz 1998, pp. 291–292. [126] Cornu 2002, p. 249.
[127] Kelényi 2003, p. 51. [128] See Bailey 2012, pp. 15–16.

before elaborating on his significance in Tibetan Buddhism. In Buddhist sūtric accounts, Rāhula is a great *asura* king who requires subjugation by the historical Buddha when he attempts to consume the sun and moon out of jealousy.[129] Once absorbed into the Tantric Buddhist tradition, Rāhula becomes especially significant in the famous *Kālacakra Tantra*, given its astrological and astronomical emphases. In this tantric cycle, Rāhula signifies the central channel of the subtle body of yogic practice, which is meant to "eclipse" the motions of the vital breath in the right (sun) and left (moon) channels.[130] Once adopted into Tibet through the assimilation of Tantric Buddhism on the plateau, Rāhula takes on far more ferocious qualities. For example, Sangyé Gyatso's *White Beryl* not only describes the planetary spirit but explains how his bodily movements change over the course of the year, and the meteorological effects that result:

> Regarding this wild *lha*, the great *ʐa* of the sky, he has nine heads topped by a tenth raven-faced one and the lower body of a coiled snake. His right hand carries a *makara*-topped victory banner and his left hand brandishes a bow and arrow made of horn. He turns onto his left side during the three months of spring and his head points west. He is face down during the three months of summer and his head points north. Regarding his face looking east, in the three autumn months his head points east and he faces south. In the three winter months his head points south and he faces west. The actions of these viewing positions [bring] rain to the earth.[131]

Other descriptions give Rāhula multiple arms, more weapons, and a body covered with a thousand eyes (Fig. 2).[132] Regardless, the above description further illustrates the close connection between dense geomantic patterns of

---

[129] See Bailey 2012, pp. 37–39. [130] See Ibid, pp. 67–68

[131] Sangs rgyas rgya mtsho 1972, p. 310.

[132] See Bailey 2012, pp. 72–73. For information on this malefic deity within the Chinese astrological and hemerological tradition, and these systems overall, see Kotyk 2017.

Figure 2 Mural of the *ʒa* (planetary) spirit Rāhula; Tengyeling Monastery, Lhasa, 2005 (photo: Christopher Bell)

the land and the shifting circumstances of seasonal time. Moreover, the deity's shifting movements are reminiscent of the *mahoraga* (*tochechenpo*) spirits of Indian demonology, giant subterranean snakes whose bodies move with the seasons and cause earthquakes. These beings belong to one of the lists for the "Eight Classes of Gods and Spirits" discussed in the Introduction. For his part, eight of Rāhula's heads are associated with these eight classes. He is also included in a group of five *sadak*, suggesting that this spirit type carries a generic quality in Tibetan astrology much like *dön* and *dre* do in the medical context.[133] Nevertheless, Rāhula offers a vivid

[133] See Nebesky-Wojkowitz 1998, p. 260.

example of how interchangeable and context-specific astrological and land spirits can be, which echoes Ramble's geometric scheme.

Hemerology

In tandem with astrological considerations are hemerological concerns that encourage or deter certain behaviors and activities throughout the lunar year. Like a Tibetan *Farmers' Almanac*, popular calendars that detail the character of auspicious and inauspicious days are published annually by the Mentsikhang, the Medical and Astrological Institute first established by the Thirteenth Dalai Lama (1876–1933). As such, the manner in which Tibetans engage with spirits across the Tibetan year differs dramatically based on the monthly occasion, the motivations of the individual, and the monastic or lay context. On a monthly basis, certain days are more prone to misfortune and spirit influences than others. For instance, the ninth, twenty-fourth, and twenty-ninth days of the month are good for performing exorcisms against evil spirits. By contrast, making offerings to divinities as well as bodhisattvas on the fifteen day will bring good fortune. A *torma* offering on the eighteenth day will help one vanquish their enemies. If someone buys a dog on the twelfth day of the month it will be a manifestation of an evil spirit. Likewise, hiring a new servant on the twenty-first day will insure they will be an evil spirit in disguise. Digging in the ground on the twenty-fifth day will anger the *lu* spirits beneath and they will cause illnesses.[134] Certain days of the week are also more appropriate than others for propitiating spirits, such as Mondays for conducting prosperity rites or Fridays for making offerings to local spirits.[135] In general, the auspiciousness of a day and the possibility of disturbing spirits are common considerations for any number of activities undertaken over the year, such as performing marriage or funerary ceremonies, embarking on a journey, building or moving into a new home, working on land, planting or cutting down trees, and even starting fights and battles.[136]

---

[134] See Karma Chagmed 1982, pp. 87–89. This article is a brief but informative collection of miscellaneous Tibetan monthly and circumstantial omens.

[135] See Cornu 2002, p. 241. [136] See Ibid, pp. 236–242.

Ritual Calendars

Tibetans also recognize a rich calendar of ceremonial and festival activities that often intersect with monastic rituals and major holy days. Such ritual and festival calendars differ by monastery and community, but a few major events are celebrated across the Tibetan plateau. The most significant holiday is the Tibetan New Year (*losar*), which is practiced according to the lunar calendar. The starting day varies from region to region, but always involves wearing new clothes, visiting with friends and family, and making offerings to deities. Historically, monastics would engage in debates and sacred dances, political officers would participate in various processions, and state oracles would fall into trance to offer prophecies for the new year. In his detailed account of premodern holidays and festivals executed throughout the year in Lhasa, Hugh Richardson describes the sacred dances performed for the Dalai Lama on the New Year and the medley of Indian and Tibetan spirits the dancers pantomime:

> They included the benevolent figures of Tshangpa, Gyachin and Namtösé (Brahma, Indra and Vaishravana); Chenmizang the Guardian King of the West, the mountain deity Chamo Zangmo, several *driza* "perfume eaters" playing flutes, woodwinds and drums; Nöjin demons; Trülbum charnelhouse ghosts; *mi* and *mimayin*, humans and non-humans; a garuda and a peacock.[137]

This ritual display is also a vivid reminder that spirits are as much a part of the world as humans and animals in the Tibetan imaginaire. That this event is presided over by the Dalai Lama, an emanation of the enlightened bodhisattva Avalokiteśvara, further situates these beings within the broader cosmic spectrum of worldly and transcendent beings.

The Tibetan New Year is quickly followed by the Great Prayer Festival (*mönlam chenmo*), preparations for which begin on the third day of the first Tibetan month and last for three weeks. This holiday was established in 1409 by Tsongkhapa Lozang Drakpa (1357–1419), founder of the Geluk

[137] Richardson 1993, p. 18.

school of Tibetan Buddhism. During the day of preparation, the Dalai Lama makes offerings to Penden Lhamo, the great Dharma protectress of not only the Geluk school but of the Dalai Lama's incarnational lineage and the city of Lhasa as well. The other protector of the Dalai Lamas, Pehar, is also beseeched on this day through the Nechung Oracle, the human medium who becomes possessed by the deity as the main state oracle that has guided the Dalai Lama's government since the seventeenth century.[138] The Nechung Oracle and other state oracles were consulted by the Tibetan government on a regular basis throughout the year for clairvoyant and prophetic advice. This most important of state oracles falls into trance several times throughout the weeks of the Great Prayer Festival, such as the tenth, fifteenth, and twenty-fourth of the month. The latter day signifies the end of festival and once involved an elaborate *torma* exorcism rite. During this ceremony a giant offering encapsulating the misfortunes of the year was shot with arrows by the Nechung Oracle while in trance before it was set ablaze.[139]

A similar exorcism rite involving the Nechung Oracle took place on the twenty-ninth day of the Second Month and is called the "Ransom Demon for the *Gyelpo*" (*lugong gyelpo*).[140] As a scapegoat ritual, this ceremony concerned one or two men who signify the ransom-offering demons that contained the misfortune for the year; they were then run out of Lhasa by the Nechung Oracle and the citizens of the city. In the process the Nechung Oracle shot arrows at another large *torma*, which was then set on fire. Because the Dalai Lama and the current Nechung Oracle lineage have lived

---

[138] See Richardson 1993, pp. 20–21. See also Bell 2013.

[139] See Richardson 1993, pp. 45–48.

[140] See Ibid, pp. 61–73; see also Imaeda 1973, Karmay 1998d, and Guidoni 1998. Richardson (1993, p. 61) translates this holiday as "Demon-Ransom King," and Karmay (1998d, p. 365) as "Ransom for the Demon-King." I agree with Karmay's understanding, with the clarification that my use of "ransom demon" refers to the *lügong* as both the ransom offering and the person carrying and representing it, who is ritually run out of town. My choice to not translate *gyelpo* as "king" retains my uniform decision to transliterate spirit types and reinforces the fact that this is a spirit being in this context, not a human ruler.

in exile since 1959, both of these ceremonies are no longer performed in Lhasa, and only meagerly in the Tibetan exile community.

A festival still celebrated annually today both inside and outside Tibet is "Incense Offerings for the Whole World" (*zamling chisang*), celebrated on the fifteenth day of the fifth lunar month. This day is specifically dedicated to making offerings to the Dharma protectors of Tibetan Buddhism, as well as to local spirits, generally by burning fragrant juniper branches. This holiday is especially important at Samyé Monastery, the first Buddhist Monastery of Tibet, where sacred dances are offered to Pehar and Tsiu Marpo, the two main protector deities of the monastery.[141] Hepori, the small mountain next to Samyé, is believed to be where the great eighth-century tantric exorcist Padmasambhava tamed the local gods and spirits so that the monastery could be constructed unencumbered by their capricious machinations. During the three days of "Incense Offerings for the Whole World," Lhasa especially becomes covered in a dense fog of incense from the hundreds of furnaces burning juniper across the city.[142] Numerous oracles traditionally fell into trance on this day as well, such as the oracles of Nechung, Darpoling, and Karmashar monasteries, all of which have some association to Pehar who is said to preside over the host of spirits being honored.[143] In Bhutan, Padmasambhava's taming of the local gods is celebrated in the eleventh month of the lunar year, where his wrathful form Dorjé Drolö is particularly revered.[144]

On the twenty-ninth day of the twelfth month, the year ends with an exorcistic rite to clear away the baneful influences of the past with a giant *torma* burning.[145] More sacred dances are performed at monasteries, fresh dough and butter offerings for the protector deities are made and installed in their chapels, and families begin preparing for the new year by cleaning and acquiring new clothes. This is also an important time to make offerings to the Dharma protectors.[146]

---

[141] See Macdonald 1978a and 1978b. I am grateful to Amy Heller for first drawing my attention to these articles.

[142] For the origins and significance of incense purification rites, see Karmay 1998e.

[143] See Richardson 1993, pp. 94–95. [144] See Cornu 2002, p. 274.

[145] See Richardson 1993, pp. 116–123. [146] See Cornu 2002, p. 275.

Beyond these major ceremonies, other holidays and deities specific to certain monasteries or sites are celebrated throughout the year. For instance, the important protector goddess Penden Lhamo was traditionally invoked on the nineteenth day of the first month as part of the Great Prayer Festival. Offerings were also made to her in the middle of the tenth month for a holiday dedicated specifically to her called "The Mountain Visit of the Glorious Goddess" (*penlhé ridra*). During this ceremony, an image of the goddess – supposedly discovered in the twelfth century – was freshly repainted and carried in procession through the Barkhor circuit around the Jokhang Temple of Lhasa. In the midst of this procession, the Karmashar Oracle in trance would offer the image a prayer scarf. Then the image of the protector deity Drip Dzongtsen would be brought out to honor the goddess, his wife, from his location at Tsechokling Monastery, just south of Lhasa across the Kyichu River.[147] For their part, images of Penden Lhamo and Drip Dzongtsen were also celebrated at the Kagyü Monastery of Tsel Gungtang southeast of Lhasa on the fifteenth day of the fourth month, where they were visited and honored by the Nechung Oracle.[148] All monasteries have their own complex ritual calendars evincing ties to various spirits and deities throughout the year.[149] These ceremonies vividly illustrate how various deities, embodied by oracles and sacred images, intersect in elaborate ways and between monastic centers for different occasions.

Many of these festivals and ceremonies also carry martial symbolism, which matches the strong warlike character of the many protector deities and spirits propitiated across Tibet.[150] For instance, on the twenty-third day of the first month a cavalry used to assemble at Lubuk in Lhasa to display their prowess with armor, weaponry, and horsemanship. Two standard-bearers joined the spectacle, with painted banners illustrating the "Red and Black Protectors of the Teachings" (*tensung marnak*), who are the main guardians of the Dalai Lamas.[151] Also, on the last day of the Great Prayer

---

[147] See Richardson 1993, pp. 30, 110–113. [148] See Ibid, pp. 87–90.

[149] See, for example, Tibetan Academy of Social Sciences 2009, pp. 460–467.

[150] See Heller 2006.

[151] See Richardson 1993, p. 34. For more on these deities and the confusion around their identities, see Heller 1990 and 1992a.

Festival, three cannons would be fired to punctuate the end of the exorcism rite; two of these cannons were named "Old and Young She-demon." As Richardson explains,

> The cannon are fired some ten times with loud reports but on the occasions that I saw the shots all fell short or wide. The mountain [shot at] is ill-omened by reason of a large heap of stones on its western end which is reputed to be the burial place of the apostate king Langdarma, and the cannonade is intended to ward off its evil influence on the city.[152]

Here, demonic forces are marshalled to empower weapons and armies in symbolic examples of military might. Spirits have been similarly incited to help ensure military success during actual battles and campaigns.[153]

In all these instances, spirits and deities are encountered at particular times for specific occasions throughout the lunar year. These engagements can pertain to rites of passage or other personal goals, such as journeys or construction projects. They can also be part of larger social systems, such as holidays, monastic ritual calendars, and communal exorcistic rites. Regardless of the circumstance, there is an implicit understanding that spirits and deities can affect the individual and community, for good or for ill, throughout the year. Tibetans are cognizant of this on a daily, monthly, and annual basis, and act accordingly in hopes of securing the protection of powerful gods or warding off the negative influences of mercurial spirits.

III Spirits and Space

Tibetan spirits are intimately tied to the landscape. Spirits like the *nyen* live among the trees and in the sky, mountain deities and *sadak* permeate the land, and *lu* ubiquitously inhabit subterranean spaces. One cannot cut down a tree, dig a ditch, or build a house without propitiating the local spirits to

---

[152] Richardson 1993, p. 49.

[153] See Gentry 2017, pp. 341–356. See also Gentry 2010, Cuevas 2019, and Yamamoto 2012, pp. 223–230.

secure their favor and avoid any negative repercussions. Two terms commonly applied to such spirits, regardless of their species, are *ʒhidak*, meaning "lord of the ground," and *yülha*, meaning "land god." Moreover, with the Tibetan plateau being so mountainous, it is not surprising that many of the spirits incorporated into regional pantheons are mountain gods who are also celebrated during annual ritual activities and festivals.

Mountain Gods

As explained in the Introduction, spirit terms often permeate names, such as the *nyen* in the name of the mountain god Nyenchen Tanglha. While these spirits were previously discussed in relation to trees, their significance is broader and more ambiguous than that. They appear to be atmospheric spirits above all, living in the spaces between the highest heavens and the surface of the earth, which would include mountains and forests. As noted earlier, the term *nyen* is often generically used to refer to spirits within this intermediate spatial domain, in contrast to the *lha* above and the *lu* below.[154] Evidence in the literature beyond this suggests that *nyen* are clan spirits as well, and since the word also refers to wild sheep or goats, it is suggestive of the animal imagery often associated with local autochthonous spirits.[155] As Karmay explains, spirit terms such as *nyen* – as well as *tsen, gyelpo, dü,* and *lu* – often make up the names or appearances of *ʒhidak* and other spirits, which speaks to the local valences of these concepts.[156] Like *nyen*, the term *tsen* also frequently stands in for spirits of the intermediate spaces. For instance, citing a Bön text, Nebesky-Wojkowitz enumerates various classes of *tsen*: "the 'rock *btsan*' (*brag btsan*) [*draktsen*], '*btsan* of the water' (*chu'i btsan*) [*chütsen*], '*btsan* of the earth' (*sa'i btsan*) [*sétsen*], '*btsan* of the sky' (*gnam btsan*) [*namtsen*], '*btsan* of the slate-mountains' (*g.ya' btsan*) [*yatsen*], 'glacier *btsan*' (*gangs btsan*) [*gangtsen*]," and so on.[157]

As previously suggested, the mountain gods also have close family connections to one another and are often described as siblings or parents to each other. The ancient Tibetan kings likewise descended from these

[154] See Karmay 1998h, pp. 441–442, and Cornu 2002, p. 248.
[155] See Karmay 1998h, p. 445. See also Karmay 1998f, pp. 420–422, and Karmay 2010.
[156] See Karmay 1998h, pp. 446–447. [157] Nebesky-Wojkowitz 1998, p. 176.

spirits, indicating the filial connection that the Tibetan people have with mountain gods. As Karmay explains, "the first [Tibetan] king is presented as the 'grandson' of the *phyva* [*cha*] deity Ya-bla bdal-drug [Yala Dendruk], and the nine mountain deities are presented as the 'sons' of the *phyva* deity 'O-lde gung-rgyal [Odé Gungyel], the fourth 'brother' of Yab-bla bdal-drug."[158] The *cha* are yet another spirit type mentioned in earlier sources but more rarely in later texts. Like the *nyen* their nature is unclear, but they appear to be atmospheric deities and are connected to the state of one's fortune. Specifically, in the context of Bön, Toni Huber explains that the *cha* are sky spirits that reside among the thirteen levels of the sky realm according to indigenous Tibetan conceptions of the layered world. While these spirits were much more extensively mentioned in imperial sources, they faded after the fifteenth century and are generally found now only within Bön enclaves in Bhutan and Arunachal Pradesh.[159] In the imperial cult, these spirits appeared to be closely associated with the *kula* and *mu*, giving the strong implication that the most ancient and autochthonous of spirit types represented different clans or groupings of deities. The relationship between these groups was complex, signifying marriage alliances and hierarchies of fealty among one another and the divine progenitors of the Tibetans. For instance, Nathan Hill argues that the *kula* were the spiritual counterpart of the Tibetan emperor originating from the land of the *mu*, while envoys from the realm of *cha* made offerings and acted as vassals.[160] The *cha* are sky gods, as Huber notes,[161] and like the *nyen* are also associated with animals in the relevant mythologies. According to one text, the son of the mountain god Odé Gungyel, who is related to both the *cha* and the *mu*, sought out a miraculous white deer that would return *cha* ("good fortune") and *yang* ("well-being") to the people, who had been stripped of such qualities by *dre*.[162] Here *cha* refers to both a spirit type and a positive attribute that can be possessed as well as lost or

---

[158] Karmay 1998h, p. 434. See also Haarh 1969, pp. 231–288.

[159] See Huber 2013, pp. 263–264.   [160] See Hill 2015, pp. 52–58.

[161] See Huber 2013, p. 264 n. 4. See also Pommaret 1994. Huber disagrees with Pommaret's claim that *cha* are mountain deities.

[162] See Berounský 2014, pp. 59–62.

stolen; it is also related to another such quality that instills well-being (*yang*), which is further associated with cattle and sheep.[163]

Several mountain gods have pan-Tibetan significance despite their local character and connection to specific mountain ranges. One such god is Yarlha Shampo, who is the ancestral deity of the Tibetan dynasty and whose mountain is located in the Yarlung Valley southeast of Lhasa, not far from where the tombs of the Tibetan emperors abide. Another mountain god, previously mentioned, is Odé Gungyel, who is the father of Yarlha Shampo and whose mountain is nearby.[164] There is also Nyenchen Tanglha, whose expansive mountain range passes through northern Tibet and who was one of the first local divinities to agree to protect the Buddhist teachings according to the Padmasambhava legends.[165] The mountain god Machen Pomra, also known as Amnye Machen, is especially significant for being closely associated with Tsongkhapa, the founder of the Geluk school. While also important among the Bön, this mountain god was Tsongkhapa's family deity, and as such its veneration was promoted by him among the Geluk. The deity's mountain range is located in Amdo, in northeast Tibet, where Tsongkhapa was born.[166] On the western edge of the Tibetan world, Mount Kailash has numerous important associations, including Padmasambhava's taming activities, Milarepa's battles with Bön sorcerers, and even connections to Sumeru, the mountain at the center of Buddhist cosmology.[167] Many mountain gods and local deities such as these find their way into institutional rituals and monastic liturgies because of their close ties to the Tibetan imperium or to important masters of various religious lineages.

Mountain gods also have strong martial characteristics in keeping with the frequent iconography of indigenous spirits as heavily armored horsemen brandishing weapons. They are often depicted as cardinal protectors in relation to one another, as illustrated by Nebesky-Wojkowitz:

---

[163] Other divinities are associated with birds, as John Bellezza explains in his exploration of Bön deities; see Bellezza 2008, pp. 332–342.

[164] See Karmay 1998e, p. 387. [165] See Nebesky-Wojkowitz 1998, p. 205.

[166] See Nebesky-Wojkowitz 1998, pp. 209–211. [167] See Ibid, pp. 223–224.

The *rMa rgyal spom ra* [Machen Pomra] of the East: a white man wearing a harness of crystal and riding on a white horse. He carries a lance with a standard and a jewel, his retinue consists of the three hundred sixty brother-deities called the *rma rigs* and of one hundred thousand *rma sman*; by the latter term apparently the consorts of the *rma* brothers are meant.

The *dByi rgyal dmag dpon* [Warlord of Yigyel] of the South: a cherry-brown man riding on a horse of the same colour, and wearing a harness of gold. His attributes are a lance with a standard and a hatchet.

The *gNyan chen thang lha* [Nyenchen Tanglha] of the West: a white man wearing a cloak and a turban of silk, riding on a quick-running bay-coloured ass. His hands hold a riding-cane and a lance with a standard.

The *sKyog chen sdang ra* [Kyokchen Dangra] ... of the North: a yellow man wearing a *srog ẓhu* [crown] and a dress of yellow silk. His mount is a swift horse with a turquoise-mane. He carries a wheel and a lance with a flag.[168]

This grouping of mountain deities is called "the four great *nyen*" (*nyenchen deẓhi*), and they are each clearly presented as warriors on horseback guarding the territory.

Luröl Festival

To this day, large spears and arrows collected and placed in cairns (*laptse*) at or near the peaks of mountains symbolize the weapons of the aforementioned divine warriors. These cairns and the giant weapons protruding from them are decorated with prayer flags and other sacred items, and they are refreshed during annual ceremonies (Fig. 3). For instance, a popular festival for the mountain gods, called Luröl,[169] is celebrated during the sixth lunar month in the mountains around the Amdo city of Rebkong in modern day Qinghai

---

[168] Nebesky-Wojkowitz 1998, p. 213.

[169] Due to Amdo dialectical differences, this festival is pronounced and usually transliterated as Laru.

province. While the festival name means "play of the *lu*," it is a celebratory time for all the local gods. Tibetans in the area will perform rituals around the mountain deity cairn and refresh its contents, local mediums will fall into oracular trances possessed by the mountain gods, and dances and other performances will be offered to the spirits in hopes that they will grant a good harvest and continue to protect the livestock.[170] Kevin Stuart, Banmadorji, and Huangchojia provide a graphic description of the dance performances that accompany these festivals to mountain gods, which often include violent activities:

> During the dances the participants circle around the dance ground; the dances are slow-paced and always performed by males. Among the dances are those in which the village leaders circle with *khadag* [prayer scarves] held in their outstretched hands, or in which the participants engage in a number of possible movements. They may, for example, hop first on the right leg then on the left; hold their real queue or artificial queue in their right hands, wave it in a circle above their heads, then at waist level; wave a length of sash in a fashion similar to that of the queue; strip to the waist, hold two sharpened spikes in their mouths, and insert two or three spikes into the flesh of the back; or dance while beating the forehead with a knife until it bleeds. Dances in which human flesh is pierced are considered an offering of flesh and blood to the gods.
>
> In the past the villagers of certain nearby communities would cut the heart out of a living goat and offer it to the mountain gods. The goat would then be burned as a sacrifice. However, such offerings ended in the late 1980s at the insistence of the Living Buddhas [incarnate lamas].[171]

---

[170] See Dpal-ldan-bkra-shis and Stuart 1998, and Stuart et al. 1995. For a more recent exploration of the Luröl Festival in light of the shifting Chinese politics surrounding the 2008 Olympics, see Makley 2018, pp. 67–104.

[171] Stuart et al. 1995, p. 233.

The authors explain that one of the mountain gods venerated during this festival in Amdo is particularly fond of goat hearts;[172] however, tensions with the Buddhist leaders of the area have led to the discontinuance of this sacrificial practice. Further south toward Sichuan, in a region called Sharkok, Samten Karmay observed a similar festival where the local men would carry large arrows up their sacred mountain and plant them in the cairn at its peak in order to reinvigorate their relationship with their mountain god. This ritual act would strengthen the deity's protection and be accompanied by singing, dancing, horse races, and – in the past – shooting contests.[173] While exploring Tibetan practices in Nepal, Stan Mumford encountered a pattern of Buddhist masters using their religious and ritual prestige to promote nonviolent practices and substitute blood offerings with dough in order to diminish the animal sacrifices common among the local communities.[174] These regional practices provide fertile ground for exploring the conflicts and negotiations that occur when religious ideals butt up against long-standing indigenous traditions.[175] Regardless, such offerings – as well as beseeching chants and pilgrimages – are performed for these mountain deities to secure their continued protection, and their military might and success is considered to be reflected in the prosperity of the region.[176]

Sadak

Spirits are also encountered on and beneath the ground, especially when a building is being constructed or wood and other materials are collected for such ventures. Proper timing and rituals are necessary to mitigate the consequences that may come from angering these spirits by encroaching on their territory. While exploring geomantic practices among Tibetan communities in Ladakh, Petra Maurer discusses how the local *sadak* – called *toché* by her informants – turns under the ground throughout

---

[172] See Stuart et al. 1995, p. 236 n. 29.   [173] See Karmay 1998g, pp. 428–429.

[174] See Mumford 1989, pp. 80–92. See also Diemberger and Hazod 1997.

[175] For a fuller discussion of the interplay between local mountain cults and Buddhism, see Denjongpa 2002.

[176] See G.yung 'brug and Rin chen rdo rje 2011. For more explorations on Tibetan mountain deities, see Blondeau and Steinkellner 1996, and Blondeau 1998. See also Bellezza 1997, Sørensen et al. 2000, Ugyen Pelgen 2007, and Dotson 2012.

Figure 3 Two large *laptse* outside of Rebkong decorated during the Luröl Festival. Giant arrows and spears are visibly jutting out from their centers. Rebkong, Qinghai, 2007 (photo: Christopher Bell)

the year. While not done in Ladakh, this spirit is drawn on the ground in other Tibetan settings before the foundation of a building can be dug. In either case, knowing the position of the underground *sadak* is important, since the groundbreaking should be done away from the spirit's face and closer to their back or stomach.[177] There are also different *sadak* for

---

[177] See Maurer 2009, p. 214. This parallels hemerological techniques for locating one's "life essence" (*la*), which moves through the body according to the phases of the moon. Medical therapies should be avoided on those days in the corresponding areas of the body where the *la* is believed to reside; see Gerke 2007, pp. 197–199. The *la* is also more vulnerable to abduction by gods or demons during certain times of the day, particularly midnight. This generally results in illness or erratic behavior

different uses of the land, whether it involves building a house, plowing a field, or establishing a charnel ground. Even married couples have a particular *sadak* associated with them, and different rituals are required for distinct occasions and circumstances.[178] The person involved in the act of digging is especially important and is not decided on a whim. As Maurer explains, "the elements (*khams*) [*kham*] of the person who digs the earth in order to lay the foundation stone should stand in a good relation to the elements of the day. His name should be a pleasing one: for example, bSod nams [Sönam], which means good fortune, merit, virtue, or something similar."[179] She cites another source explaining that the digger should also be born in the pig year, likely because it is considered especially fortuitous. Where one is born likewise has a *sadak* that presides over the land, and by extension the well-being of the person. When someone falls ill and an oracular healer is entreated, they may have to make offerings to the *sadak* of the person's natal land before ministering to their health.[180]

Site consecrations are equally important at monasteries and retreat centers so that practitioners can delineate or maintain the sacred spaces in which their more soteriologically oriented practices take place. In examining the earth ritual as it pertains to constructing a Buddhist *maṇḍala*, Cathy Cantwell explains that after the land is requested from the *sadak*, the Earth Goddess herself will be propitiated in an intentional reflection of the Buddha Śākyamuni calling the earth to witness and defeating the demonic god Māra before achieving enlightenment. More offerings are then made to earth spirits and other minor divinities before advanced meditational exercises are performed to secure the area.[181] Such an elaborate tantric ritual speaks to the Indian origin of groundbreaking ceremonies in Tibet, which were nevertheless also influenced by China, like the plateau's astrological system.

and ransom rituals must be performed to retrieve the stolen or lost *la*; see Karmay 1998c, pp. 314–315.

[178] See Maurer 2009, pp. 214–215.   [179] Ibid, p. 214.

[180] Personal correspondence with a Tibetan associate; Lhasa, November 24, 2011.

[181] See Cantwell 2005, pp. 6–12. For more on specifically monastic interactions with local gods, see Mills 2003, pp. 243–262, and Sneath 2007. For more on *sadak* and their connection to divination and geomancy, see Schuh 2012 and 2013.

The Tibetan landscape is vast. With an expansive sky, seemingly endless chains of mountains, and fickle weather and waterways, it is understandable that there would be equally fickle spirits embodying and inhabiting these realms. Encountering and interacting with the spirits that fill these spaces is inevitable, which is why a range of ritual etiquette exists to appease and cooperate with them. Beyond a close connection with individual bodies and seasonal time, the dimensions of space are equally important in understanding how Tibetans engage with the numerous kinds of spirits that inhabit the plateau and the world at large. This further ties into a greater foundational concept found in the Tibetan imaginaire: the notion of place and its concentric sacrality. A popular example of this is the Jokhang Temple in Lhasa, which is circumambulated by Tibetans in ever-widening circuits in relation to the sacred statue at its center. Likewise, certain landscapes are considered more naturally auspicious than others, either as hidden lands, pilgrimage sites, or prophetically significant religious centers.[182] Spirits inhabit all of these spaces as steadfast protectors of monasteries, unyielding gatekeepers of valleys, and even as bloodthirsty bandits in need of bribing.

IV Spirits and Doctrine

Many of the examples given so far portray spirits as fairly generic, belonging to various numbered groupings, or representing territories and regions without much character. However, most of these beings have rich mythologies that evince a strong personality only captured in local accounts or available in religious records. Given their ability to preserve and retain such narratives, it is often only in institutional rituals and historical collections that specific spirits and deities are described in detail when oral tales are scant or limited in audience. Moreover, there is a robust heritage of local spirits being subjugated by Buddhist or Bön masters, sometimes violently, in order to serve and protect the religious

---

[182] For more on the sacred nature of space and pilgrimage in Tibet, see Dowman 1988, Huber 1999a and 1999b, Gutschow and Ramble 2003, and Childs 2004, pp. 74–97.

communities to which they are now beholden. These spirits are usually called "Dharma protectors" (*chökyong*) or "guardians" (*sungma*), and, as explained in the Introduction, these titles include both transcendent and worldly deities.

The most famous Buddhist subjugation narrative concerns the important eighth-century tantric master Padmasambhava traveling across the Himalayas and Tibetan Plateau taming the autochthonous deities in the service of Buddhism by emulating tantric tutelary deities. Accounts of Padmasambhava's exploits go back to Tibet's dark age (late ninth century), but the famed twelfth-century treasure-revealer Nyangrel Nyima Özer (1124–1192) was the first to develop a full biography of this important figure before it was extensively elaborated upon in the fourteenth century by the treasure-revealer Ogyan Lingpa (b. 1323).[183] The degree of detail aside, these biographies all describe Padmasambhava forcefully subduing local goddesses, mountain gods, and capricious spirits. The divinities are then added to the complex *maṇḍalas* of dense tantric cycles and are often perceived as residing in the courtyards of these numinous spaces. Similar accounts also exist of the Bön founder Shenrap Miwo, who encountered the numerous gods of the land and press-ganged them into protecting the Bön doctrine.[184] In several cases, Buddhist and Bön protector deities have nearly identical names, iconographies, and origins, which speaks to the institutional sharing that takes place between these narratives.[185] The institutional religions of Tibet are powerful in part because they dominate the capricious forces of the landscape and use them to protect and defend their traditions. In Tibetan mythic history this concept even predates

---

[183] For a detailed exploration of Padmasambhava's mythic and biographical significance, see Hirshberg 2016. See also Dalton 2004 and Cantwell and Mayer 2013. For Ogyan Lingpa's biography of Padmasambhava, see O rgyan gling pa 1996. The first major translation of this work into a European language was produced in French by Gustave-Charles Toussaint; see Toussaint 1933. A flawed but useful English translation of Toussaint's text was then produced almost half a century later; see Douglas and Bays 1978.

[184] See Bellezza 2010 and Snellgrove 1967, pp. 42–97. For more on the sharing of these biographical narratives, see Haarh 1969, pp. 319–320.

[185] For examples, see Blezer 2004 and Bell 2006, pp. 147–149. For broader studies on Bön deities, see Kvaerne 1990 and 2007, as well as Mori 2004.

Padmasambhava, when the first Buddhist King Songtsen Gampo was believed to establish thirteen temples across the plateau in order to physically pin down the giant demoness that constitutes the land of Tibet. It was Songtsen Gampo's Chinese wife, Princess Wencheng (623?-680), who first envisioned Tibet as a demoness, having used Chinese divination to ascertain the difficulties she had encountered on her journey to the plateau.[186] That fierce spirits were reoriented to guard the Buddhist and Bön teachings and their communities is a foundational aspect of Tibetan religious history, and one with explicitly tantric roots.

Spirit Subjugation

The most famous account of enlightened beings forcefully taming a wrathful demonic spirit is found in the Buddhist *Gathering of Intentions Sūtra*, where a powerful demon named Rudra is defeated by wrathful tantric divinities such as Vajrapāṇi and Hayagrīva.[187] In this story, Rudra was well meaning and devout in an earlier incarnation, but over time his religious practice became debased while his friend's practice improved. As he worsened and became jealous of his friend's success, he grew more wrathful, until over several lifetimes he was reborn in increasingly ferocious forms. Eventually, he became the terrifying king of demons. His friend, meanwhile, became Vajrapāṇi, and he and other enlightened figures gradually took over Rudra's kingdom and overpowered him through the use of violent forms. At one climactic point in the narrative, accounts graphically describe Hayagrīva shrinking to a miniscule size, entering Rudra's anus, and expanding from within the demon's belly in order to explode outward. Indeed, Hayagrīva as a horse-headed deity is commonly shown wearing Rudra's body like clothes, his equine head(s)

---

[186] See Gyatso 1987, Miller 1998, Marko 2003, and Mills 2007. See also Gyaltsen 1996, pp. 163–187, and Sørensen 1994, pp. 251–297.

[187] Jacob Dalton provides a thorough examination and complete translation of the Rudra myth as presented in chapters 20–31 of the *Gathering of Intentions Sūtra* in his study of the myth's significance and relationship to violence in Tibetan Buddhism; see Dalton 2011, pp. 159–206. See also Stein 1995, Mayer 1998, Davidson 2003, and Dalton 2016.

protruding from the demon's forehead.[188] In the end, Rudra is subjugated and converted to Buddhism to act as a guardian of the religion. This foundational mythology is rife with classic tantric activity and imagery, such as wrathful enlightened beings, antinomian violence, and powerful ritual technologies of subjugation. Several scholars have further argued that the structure and tropes of the Rudra myth inspired the origin accounts for many of the Dharma protectors of Tibetan Buddhism.[189]

The mythography of protector deities further evinces the escalating layers of domination that ritual masters utilize to overpower capricious spirits. The relevant Tibetan texts often speak of "four activities" (*trinlé namzhi*) that Padmasambhava, and later exorcists emulating him, implemented in order to successfully subdue recalcitrant gods and demons. These four activities are pacification, enrichment, subjugation, and destruction. When dealing with problematic spirits, a ritual specialist will work through these activities one by one until the result is successful. For instance, the specialist will first attempt to quell the wrathful forces of the spirit through pacification rites. If that fails, they will attempt to bribe them or counteract their negative influences by augmenting the fortune of the afflicted family, community, or locale. Failing that, more direct and violent taming rituals will be performed. Finally, if all else fails lethal rites will be conducted in effort to ultimately destroy the spirit and send them onto a better rebirth.[190] An infamous example of this is connected to the controversial deity Dorjé Shukden, who is considered to be the wrathful reincarnation of the seventeenth-century Geluk master Drakpa Gyentsen (1619–1656). According to popular tradition, the Fifth Dalai Lama, with the aid of Nyingma lamas, attempted to destroy this spirit as he was causing disturbances and proving to be obstinate against other ritual actions. The destructive rite ultimately failed, it seems, though there is much debate over its veracity and significance.[191]

---

[188] For a summary account, see Kapstein 2000, pp. 170–174. See also O rgyan gling pa 1996, pp. 29–56.

[189] See Stein 1995, Dalton 2011, pp. 59–73, and Bailey 2017, pp. 207–214.

[190] See Cuevas 2015, pp. xxi–xxiv, and Gentry 2017, pp. 336–341.

[191] See Dreyfus 1998, p. 239. See also Nebesky-Wojkowitz 1998, pp. 134–144, and McCune 2007.

Regardless, it is a vivid example of how other masters after Padmasambhava's time have acted to subdue capricious spirits. This ties into a popular Tibetan belief that Padmasambhava's subjugation of local spirits was unfinished, which is why even protector deities need to be constantly propitiated and reminded of their vow to guard the Dharma.[192]

Dharma Protectors

Myths regarding Padmasambhava's taming of local spirits and entrusting them to serve as maintainers of the Buddhist teachings and community act as a ready model for later and contemporary masters to follow. The common narrative structure found in the relevant accounts concern him traveling through Tibet, encountering spirits, and awing them with his spiritual prowess before compelling them, sometimes violently, to act for the good of the Dharma. One ready example can be found in the *Chronicle of Gods and Demons*, where Padmasambhava meets and tames an important group of local goddesses in Tsang:

> Then [Padmasambhava] went to Dremona in Uyuk, where he subjugated the Twelve Tenma Goddesses of Central and East Tibet and scattered them between two mountains. The master went into the sky and lotus flowers appeared; thus there were miraculous signs. [The goddesses said,] "We request good fortune so we will not create obstacles! We take refuge at your feet and will not harm you!" [The goddesses] offered their life essence and [Padmasambhava] bound them under oath and skillfully entrusted them with a treasure text.[193]

Padmasambhava proceeds to subdue other goddesses associated with mountains and assigns them treasures to protect. Similar encounters with spirits are even illustrated on monastery murals. One especially vivid portrayal is found on the walls of the Tsangpa Chapel in Meru Sarpa Monastery, Lhasa, which

---

[192] See Diemberger 2007.

[193] O rgyan gling pa 1997, p. 39. See also Blondeau 1971, p. 32. For more on this important group of goddesses, see Nebesky-Wojkowitz 1998, pp. 181–198.

shows Padmasambhava taming the god Pehar. In these murals, Pehar first attempts to frighten and distract the tantric master by transforming into a ferocious lion, upending his ritual objects, and dropping a meteor on his head. None of these tactics work, however, and Padmasambhava retaliates by using various powerful *mudrās* against the deity before finally receiving the deity's life essence and conferring empowerments upon him.[194]

With popular deities, these murals and related texts provide detailed discussions of their mythic origins and impact on Tibetan history. For his part, once subjugated Pehar was made into the protector of the treasury at Samyé Monastery. Prior to this, however, he had been a devout king who became ordained. Like Rudra, his practice eventually deteriorated, and he became a mighty and violent demon king who terrorized the world with his team of five spirits before being subdued.[195] The other major protector of Samyé, Tsiu Marpo, had a similar origin (Fig. 4). He had been a prince of Khotan and a monk, before a local king wanted to have him killed. The trauma of this caused Tsiu Marpo's monastic vows to falter and he died violently and in a wrathful state of mind. He was reborn as a demonic being who tormented the world and headed a team of seven spirit riders that were eventually tamed by Padmasambhava.[196] Other demons-turned-protectors were subjugated either by earlier tantric divinities, like the protector Begtse,[197] or by later masters, like the three ferocious Sakya Witches,[198] as well as the controversial Dorjé Shukden. An observably common pattern with many protector deities is that they are the spirits of past mythic or historical human figures, the origins of which Erik Haarh traces back to pre-Buddhist Tibetan anxieties over the spirits of the deceased.[199]

---

[194] See Bell 2017.

[195] For an extensive exploration of Pehar's myths and cult, see Bell 2013. See also Nebesky-Wojkowitz 1998, pp. 94–133, and Grenet 2000.

[196] For more on this protector deity, see Bell 2006. See also Nebesky-Wojkowitz 1998, pp. 166–176. Amy Heller also discusses Tsiu Marpo extensively in her doctoral thesis; see Heller 1992b.

[197] For more on Begtse, see Heller 1988, 1990, 1992a, and 1992b. See also Nebesky-Wojkowitz 1998, pp. 88–93.

[198] See Conrad 2012. [199] See Haarh 1969, pp. 321–322.

Figure 4 Central statue of Tsiu Marpo at Tengyeling Monastery, satellite of Samyé Monastery, Lhasa 2011 (photo: Cecilia Haynes)

Regarding Dorjé Shukden, the debate centers around his ontological status; most Tibetans and Tibetan Buddhists see him as a pernicious spirit while a minority believe he is an enlightened being. Much of the tension stems from this spirit being perceived as especially sectarian, violently striking down Geluk masters who "tarnish" the tradition's teachings with that of other schools. An infamous collection of such accounts, popularly known as the *Yellow Book* and published in the 1970s,[200] relates how the Eighth Panchen Lama

---

[200] This text, which was composed by Dzemé Rinpoche (Dze smad sprul sku 04 Blo bzang dpal ldan bstan 'dzin yar rgyas, 1927–1996), is actually entitled the *Swelling Roar of Amassed Clouds of Nectar and Black Clouds Flickering with Nooses of Fearsome Lightning: The Teachings of the Capable Father Lama Conveying the Origins of the*

(1854/1855–1882) not only mixed his practice by studying Nyingma texts but actively slighted the deity, which the book claims led to his early demise:

> By way of a proper symbolic representation of actually forcing the Dharma protector [Dorjé Shukden] himself into the sacrificial fire, [the Eighth Panchen Lama] burned that very *tangka* [painted scroll of the deity] in the hearth of a fire *pūjā* together with other fire offerings. Other than becoming permeated with ghee oil, for example, the *tangka* was not in fact burned by the fire, but it was removed from the hearth and defiled by many bad substances. He also pressed the *tangka* beneath the doorstep of his apartment at Tashi Lhünpo Monastery. Because he performed such destructive rites, this Panchen Rinpoche, having reached the age of thirty, took ill in the Water-Sheep year of the fifteenth sexagenarian cycle [1883] and passed away. On top of this, a terrifying well-dressed monk with a beard appeared in his apartment and displayed many magical illusions.[201]

Dorjé Shukden is a special case, however, and most protectors are highly revered within their lineages, with some having especially close ties to a distinct school. One famous protector named Achi Chökyi Drölma even began her life as the great-grandmother of Jikten Sumgön (1143–1217), the founder of the Drikung Kagyü school. She was apotheosized by the tradition and considered an emanation of the female Buddha Vajrayoginī, which speaks to the diffuse boundaries that can exist between transcendent and worldly deities.[202] King Gesar of Ling is another important protector, with a rich indigenous history of folk stories and bardic lineages offering captivating accounts of this great warrior as he defeats demons across the plateau.[203]

Great Protector of the Teachings, Mighty Dorjé Shukden, who is Great with Power and Strength; see Blo bzang dpal ldan 1973.

[201] Blo bzang dpal ldan 1973, pp. 9–10.   [202] See Muldowney 2011.

[203] For more on Gesar, see Penick 1996, Samuel 1995, FitzHerbert 2015, Kornman et al. 2015, and Mikles 2016.

The origins and stories of Dharma protectors are often scattered across various ritual collections and histories tied to certain institutions. However, a particularly famous anthology of protector biographies is the eighteenth-century *Unprecedented Elegant Explanation Briefly Expounding the Hagiographies and Iconographies of the Ocean of Oath-Bound Guardians of the Teachings*,[204] composed by the Geluk master Lelung Jedrung Zhepé Dorjé (1697–1740). This work is especially thorough in recording the sources Lelung drew from to compile his accounts, though it has a Geluk bent given the author's background.[205] In English, Réne de Nebesky-Wojkowitz's *Oracles and Demons of Tibet* continues to be the most comprehensive treatment on protector deities, despite being more than sixty years old.

It is in the protector chapels (*gönkang*) of monasteries and temples that one will encounter the local character and significance of these divinities. In these shrine rooms the walls are often covered in gory imagery and desolate scenery, and further lined with murals, *tangka* paintings, and statues of the protectors connected to that institution's spiritual lineage, masters, and geographical sites.[206] These images provide a robust iconographic history for the religious center. For instance, at Nechung Monastery where the protector deity Pehar eventually comes to reside, the inner sanctum has statues of him and the group of deities he leads, the goddesses associated with the Geluk ritual corpus, a protector goddess of the land named Nyima Zhönnu, and a statue of the subjugating tantric deity Hayagrīva with his consort. For Nechung in particular, this rich network of divinities radiates out to the monastery assembly hall, where murals of Pehar and his deities are found alongside Padmasambhava, Hayagrīva, and enlightened tantric beings associated with the Nyingma school called the Eight Proclamation deities, to be discussed below. Finally, the courtyard itself is covered in murals of dozens of lesser spirits in Pehar's entourage rising over an ocean of blood. This imagery creates a powerful atmosphere as well as a sense of movement as one makes

---

[204] The Tibetan title of this text is *dam can bstan srung rgya mtsho'i rnam par thar pa cha shas tsam brjod pa sngon med legs bshad.*

[205] See Bzhad pa'i rdo rje 1976, 1978, 1979, and 2003. See also Bailey 2017 and 2019b.

[206] See Lozang Jamspal 2006 and Ricca and Fournier 1996.

their way deeper into the monastery, first passing a retinue of capricious worldly spirits before moving toward the wrathful protector himself and related guardians, all under the watchful gaze of fierce enlightened beings.[207] Nechung is unique for its ubiquitous spirit imagery, but all monasteries and temples have some shrine room or space dedicated to propitiating Dharma protectors. Beyond the images, these protector chapels are often further decorated with weapons such as spears and arrows, the pelts of wolves and tigers, and fierce masks along the banners and pillars. The wrathful protectors especially enjoy alcohol (*chang*) and meat – offered to them by lay patrons as well as the local monastics – and their heady scent permeates the air, mingling with the waxy smell of yak butter lamps. Because of their ferocious and powerful atmosphere, these chapels are often restricted to women and outsiders. Nonetheless, monastics and laity alike engage with the spirits of these spaces through a rich system of ritual manuals, divinatory practices, and devotional activities, all of which take place at religious centers and sacred sites, or, in private homes.

Conclusion

It is one thing to attempt to classify spirits, as Tibetans and scholars of Tibet have done, and another to interact with these beings. Tibetan spirits fit different categorical schemes and interrelational designations, which makes delimiting the boundaries of Tibetan demonology difficult. While this Element has attempted to draw such an otherwise arbitrary boundary – distinguishing Tibetan spirit types from humans and enlightened beings – the lines between these labels are ontologically blurry in practice. Several examples herein illustrate that many wrathful spirits are those of humans who died violently; Dharma protectors can be considered worldly spirits by some and enlightened beings by others, or even originate from tantric tutelary deities; and converted local spirits often crowd the cosmic courtyards of *maṇḍalas*. The "Eight Classes" (*degyé*) of gods and demons are themselves often treated as the worldly reflection of the transcendent and tantric "Eight Proclamation" deities (*kagyé*), first enumerated and elaborated upon in the

---

[207] See Bell 2013, pp. 176–187.

twelfth century by Nyangrel Nyima Özer.[208] In monastic chapels and institutional catalogs, protector deities and their entourages of indigenous spirits are ensconced within larger cosmic arrays of frightening tantric divinities and powerful religious masters.[209] In rituals collected within the works of prolific religious figures it is common to find high liturgies to tantric and enlightened beings followed immediately by rites to lesser protector deities before ending with apotropaic texts for controlling or warding off untamed local spirits. Tibetan spirits are part of a greater universe that runs the gamut from the play of the buddhas to the mundane concerns of the populace. The manner in which monastics and laity alike propitiate and interact with these beings is equally diverse, so giving summary attention to the ritual activities that have been encountered in different contexts above will provide a fitting epilogue to this work.

Approaching the Spirits

Religious sites in Tibet have historically been the center of a rich variety of ritual activity. These activities include daily, monthly, and annual recitations, *torma* offerings, statue consecrations, thread-cross rites, ritual dances, oracle possessions, and festivals, as well as rituals connected to other institutions. Despite their diversity of execution, all of these rituals are

---

[208] These "Eight Proclamation" deities are the central Heruka deities of the Nyingma Mahāyoga scriptural tradition. They are: (1) Yamāntaka, deity of the body (*'jam dpal sku gshin rje shed*); (2) Hayagrīva, deity of speech (*pad ma gsung rta mgrin*); (3) Viśuddha, deity of the mind (*yang dag thugs*); (4) Vajrāmṛta, deity of good qualities (*rdo rje bdud rtsi yon tan*); (5) Vajrakīlāya, deity of activities (*rdo rje phur ba 'phrin las*); (6) Mātara, deity of invoking and dispatching (*ma mo rbod gtong*); (7) Lokastotrapujanātha, deity of mundane offerings and praises (*'jig rten mchod bstod*); and (8) Mantrabhīru, deity of wrathful mantras (*dmod pa drag sngags*). The details of these deities are found in the treasure collection discovered by Nyangrel Nyima Özer entitled the *Assembly of the Sugatas of the Eight Proclamations (Bka' brgyad bde gshegs 'dus pa)*. See Tenzin Samphel 2008 and Grizman 2016.

[209] For iconographically vivid portrayals of this ontological progression of Indo-Tibetan pantheons, see Getty 1962, Lohia 1994, Willson and Brauen 2000, and Chandra and Bunce 2002. See also Mills 2003, pp. 185–189.

necessary tools for engaging with protector deities and Tibetan spirits in general. The periodic recitation of ritual manuals (*kangso*) is at the core of most major performances, from thread-cross construction to oracular possession, since each of these activities requires a vocal invocation to consecrate the sacred object or summon important deities. The number of monks, the length of the recitation, and the degree to which it is accompanied by musical instrumentation and ritual implements may change depending on the circumstances and occasion, but the basic goals are the same.[210]

Torma offerings often accompany ritual recitations, especially lengthier ceremonies. Such offerings are presented to the monastery's deities in the course of a ritual and in elaborate configurations consistent with the spirit category to which the deities belong.[211] *Tormas* made and offered for specific occasions are usually discarded after the ritual is complete; however, there are also year-long or continuous *tormas* constructed and preserved near or on the altars of the deities. These *tormas* act as constant offerings to the monastery's deities and are replaced only once a year, usually as part of the New Year festivities. Temporary and continuous *tormas* must be consecrated with mantras provided in the pertinent ritual manuals before they can be presented to the deities, whose presence is believed to be made manifest through the ritual process as well as within the locus of their statues and murals. Beyond *tormas*, other offerings such as barley beer (*chang*), milk, yogurt, and butter lamps are occasionally presented at the altar in front of or near the deities' statues by monastics and laity.

The sacred images and statues housed in monasteries have all been consecrated through ritual recitation and mantric invocation.[212] The completion of this process is the "eye-opening ceremony" (*chenyewé choga*), which

---

[210] For more on these important ritual collections, see Mills 2003, pp. 185–205, and Pommaret 2007.

[211] For lists and drawings of specific *tormas* and the spirit types to which they are generally offered, see Nebesky-Wojkowitz 1998, pp. 343–354, and Beer 2004, pp. 320–335.

[212] For the most detailed examination of this consecration process as it pertains to images and reliquaries, see Bentor 1996.

involves painting the eyes of the *tangka* image, mural, or statue in order to sacralize the object. Consecration allows the statue to act as a suitable offering and vessel for the deity, which in turn makes it a fitting locus to which *tormas* and other offerings can be given. These images are spatial manifestations of the spirits in contrast to their temporal manifestations exhibited during periodic ritual recitations. This constant visual presence is also used by the monks to aid their mental visualization of the deities during ritual performances. Thread-cross mansions further act as physical expressions of important deities. These geometric constructions are small models of the deity's divine mansion; each consists of sticks and colored thread and can stand two to six feet in height.[213] Just as statues act as a spatial manifestation of the deity, thread-cross mansions act as a spatial manifestation of their divine abode.

Ritual dances have also been an important element of the religious life of all major Tibetan monasteries. The practice has diminished severely in Tibet since the mid-twentieth century, but it is still done today at historically important sacred centers, such as Samyé Monastery. These dances reenact the great mythic stories of Padmasambhava and other tantric exorcists in their efforts to subdue the local gods and spirits, and also illustrate the activities of the higher Buddhist gods and enlightened beings. During these narrative performances, which can last for many hours over many days, monks wear masks and dress in costumes signifying various gods, exorcists, and tutelary deities. As representations of important protector deities, the monks perform specific dance routines around or for a central figure. These routines are accompanied by music and tell a story of conflict, subjugation, and, ultimately, liberation.

Oracular possession is yet another extensive ritual engagement with spirits, bringing them directly into the presence of monastics, the community, or even the Dalai Lama's government. Once offerings are made to the deities through the oracles as part of a ritual program, they are asked to aid the monastery, the government, or Tibet at large. After a deity descends into a medium, they respond to questions and provide prophetic advice to those present.

---

[213] For a fuller exploration of these and other Tibetan thread-cross structures, see Nebesky-Wojkowitz 1998, pp. 369–397, as well as Blondeau 1990 and 2004.

Overall, diverse ritual activities maintain an active relationship with the gods and spirits. It is important to note that these different rituals are not mutually exclusive but, rather, are mutually reinforcing; they are often performed together on many occasions. Oracle sessions are accompanied by ritual recitations and often include *torma* offerings; the same is true for ritual dances. The timing and configuration of these ritual programs are established over the course of the Tibetan year and make up regional ritual calendars.[214]

A popular ritual practice through which spirits can also be entreated is divination (*mo*). Divinatory practices range from basic acts to complex ceremonies and can be done by laypersons, hired diviners, or monastic authorities, depending on the circumstances. Chime Radha Rinpoche gives a cogent explanation for divination's spectrum of utility:

> Recourse to divination might be had about any of the important events and decisions of life: the arranging of marriages, the birth of children, the undertaking of journeys and affairs of business, the choice of site for building a house, the treatment of sickness and disease, the outcome of legal disputes, the recovery of lost articles and animals, social relationships, plans and ambitions of all kinds, and indeed any matter about which a person felt sufficiently anxious to wish to have some reassurance or forewarning in advance of the actual outcome of events.[215]

The means of foretelling such concerns are just as varied. The easiest method is rosary divination, which can be done without a specialist. A random length of beads is held in one's hand, counted off in threes, and the remaining number is counted and interpreted favorably (if it is an odd number) or unfavorably (if it is an even number).[216] Other methods include using dice,

---

[214] For an excellent exploration of Tibetan ritual that offers diverse methodological approaches, see Cabezón 2010.

[215] Chime Radha Rinpoche 1981, pp. 4–5.

[216] See Ekvall 1963, pp. 34–35. For an alternative method of interpretation based on counting by fours, see Chime Radha Rinpoche 1981, p. 15.

pebbles, butter lamps, songs, arrows, mirrors or reflective surfaces, and divination cards.[217] Bird divination is also popular, where the behavior and specific sounds of ravens and crows are interpreted as certain types of omens.[218] Even scapulimancy has been observed among Tibetan communities; this is where a sheep's shoulder blade is placed in a fire until it cracks, then the cracks are read for signs.[219] For a number of these methods, a divination manual is required to properly interpret the results of the forecast, since it lists all possible results and their meanings. Dreams can also act as powerful portents, especially around significant times of the year or during important life junctures. Astrology is often used alongside these various types of divination in order to determine auspicious or inauspicious times and days for certain activities. All of these methods provide a means for recognizing certain omens in order to come to an informed decision.[220]

Another popular form of prediction is mirror divination. This can be performed with a hand-held mirror or another reflective surface, including the surface of a lake. This was once one of the primary forms of prophesying the next rebirth of the Dalai Lama. The regent and other officials would go specifically to Lhamo Lhatso Lake, southeast of Lhasa, and see a vision in the lake's reflection that showed the site of the Dalai Lama's rebirth. This lake is believed to be the soul lake of the enlightened goddess Penden Lhamo.[221] The same principle is applied to hand-held mirrors: diviners see visions reflected in a mirror in response to queries they recite out loud. This is usually preceded by panegyrics to a specific deity, such as Gesar or Dorjé Yudrönma, who is believed to provide the vision.[222]

---

[217] For more information on dice divination in particular, see Dotson 2007, 2015, and 2018; for Tibetan cartomancy, see Stein 1939; for lithomancy, see Smith 2015. For a more recent exploration of dice and bead divination, see Sobisch and Nielsen 2019. See also Maurer, et al. 2020.

[218] See Laufer 1914, Mortensen 2003, and Nishida 2013.

[219] See Nebesky-Wojkowitz 1998, pp. 455–456, Walter 1996, and Nishida 2016

[220] For a dated but still informative description of Tibetan divination, see Waddell 1973, pp. 105–115; see also Nielsen 2018.

[221] See Chime Radha Rinpoche 1981, p. 10, and Diemberger 2005, pp. 133–136.

[222] See Nebesky-Wojkowitz 1998, pp. 462–463, and Orofino 1994.

Divination is just as often used to discover something concealed in the past as it is to reveal the future. For instance, a Tibetan colleague of mine explained that in 2008, a large cyst had begun to grow on his neck just below his chin. Medical aid was of no use, so his mother contacted a *mantric* specialist (*ngakpa*). The specialist used divination to determine the cause, which was that my colleague had eaten some impure meat. Thinking back, he recalled accidently eating frog meat while he was in Beijing and he thought this must have been the cause. He met the specialist, who reconfirmed the cause through rosary divination, and began a lengthy treatment regimen that ultimately cured the cyst.

Regardless of the popularity and ubiquity of divination in Tibetan communities, many monks today tend to look down on the practice as superstitious. This may in part be due to the indigenous and non-Buddhist nature of many of these methods. Though they are often called upon to perform these services for laymen and women, monks sometimes chide devotees for not putting greater faith in the buddhas and enlightened masters, or for not fully understanding the consequences of their own karma.[223]

Speaking of Demons

The amorphous nature of Tibetan divinities across the Buddhist and Bön, lay and monastic spectrum could in many ways be considered analogous to language, which also cannot be essentialized. Tibetan demonologies attempt to communicate a collection of constantly shifting and multivalent symbols in order to make sense of the world. These symbols are anthropomorphic "sentences" that share modules of semiotic significance – such as coloration, iconography, weaponry, mythology, narrative history, textual tradition, ritual activity, and locality. However, they are combined in different permutations across networks of meaning and interpreted in different ways to signify unique instances by which to express shared ideas. Like language, these ideas are developed organically in local settings, and only after the fact is an artificial and incomplete structure applied to them that can never quite encompass the whole, always having to make room for countless exceptions that foil efforts to define and delimit. Consider the shifting taxonomy of demonic species and the fluctuating

---

[223] Mikmar Tsering, personal communication, November 20, 2011.

hierarchies of various deities along worldly or transcendent classes, not to mention malevolent and tantric designations. Like language, there are also many regional variations and idiomatic forms that are constantly changing, frustrating comprehension and making complete fluency illusory. Languages are likewise based on relation and location, and the intersections of meaning between words, syntax, and grammar is always in flux. Just as language is important in the process of attempting to make sense of a given society, so too is this vernacular of the gods essential in gaining a greater understanding of Tibetan culture and religion. It is important to study Tibetan gods and spirits, where they come from, how they are understood and evolve, what rituals they are associated with, and how they influence diverse Tibetan social responses. While this drudgery demonic can seem intimidating, it offers us deeper insights into the richness of Tibetan religious expression.

Tibetan Transliteration and Translation

Today, the Tibetan script is generally transliterated into Latin letters using the standard system of Tibetan transcription established by Turrell Wylie sixty years ago.[1] Since the Wylie transliteration scheme accounts for the many silent prefixes, superscripts, subscripts, suffixes, and secondary suffixes that can make up a Tibetan syllable, it is useful for scholars and specialists who want to reverse engineer the meaning and proper pronunciation of the original Tibetan. However, the system is not helpful for nonspecialists, who are otherwise stymied in their pronunciation attempts by the seemingly extra consonants and vague apostrophes that tumble over one another. To remedy this obscurity, David Germano and Nicolas Tournadre developed an incredibly useful Simplified Phonetic Transcription of Standard Tibetan for the Tibetan and Himalayan Library at the start of the twenty-first century.[2] One limitation of this system is that it phonetically renders Tibetan words in accordance with the central Tibetan dialect. Nonetheless, I rely on this transcription scheme to make Tibetan names and words more accessible to the general reader, while providing a glossary at the end of the Element that provides equivalent Wylie transliterations for specialists. All translations from French and Tibetan are my own unless otherwise stated.

[1] See Wylie 1959. [2] See Germano and Tournadre 2003.

Glossary

Term	Tibetan Wylie Transliteration
Achi Chökyi Drölma	a phyi chos kyi sgrol ma
Amdo	a mdo
Amnye Machen	a myes rma chen
Barrarotsa	'bar ba ro tsa
Begtse	beg tse
Blue Beryl	*baidūrya sngon po*
Bön	bon
cha	phywa
cham	'chams
chang	chang
Changtang	byang thang
chenyewé choga	spyan dbye ba'i cho ga
Chokgyur Lingpa	mchog gyur gling pa
chöjé	chos rje
chökyong	chos skyong
Chronicle of Gods and Demons	*lha 'dre bka' thang*
chudre	chu 'dre
chungsi	chung sri
chütsen	chu'i btsan
damsi	dam sri
Darpoling	dar po gling
degyé	sde brgyad
denma	dal ma
dön	gdon
Dörjé Drolö	rdo rje gro lod

dorjé düpa	rdo rje mdud pa
Dorjé Shukden	rdo rje shugs ldan
Dorjé Yudrönma	rdo rje g.yu sgron ma
dra	dgra
Drakpa Gyentsen	grags pa rgyal mtshan
draktsen	brag btsan
dralha	dgra lha
drangsong	drang srong
Drashenjin	sgra gshan 'jin
dre	'dre
drekpa	dregs pa
dri	dri
Drikung	'bri gung
drip	grib
Drip Dzongtsen	grib rdzong btsan
driza	dri za
drupa	grub pa
dü	bdud
durtrö dre	dur khrod 'dre
Duwajukring	du ba mjug ring
Four Tantras	*rgyud bzhi*
Gadong	dga' gdong
gangtsen	gangs btsan
Gathering of Intentions Sūtra	*dgongs pa 'dus pa'i mdo*
gek	bgegs
gekdröl	bgegs dkrol
Geluk	dge lugs
gen	rgan
gödre	god 'dre
gongpo	'gong po

gönkang	mgon khang
gowé lhanga	'go ba'i lha lnga
Gyajin	brgya byin
gyelgong	rgyal 'gong
gyelpo	rgyal po
gyelsi	rgyal sri
Hepori	has po ri'
Jangöndrakpo	ljang sngon drag po
jetem	byad stems
jiktenledepé sungma	'jig rten las 'das pa'i srung ma
jiktenpé sungma	'jig rten pa'i srung ma
Jikten Sumgön	'jig rten gsum mgon
Jinuratsa	byi nu ra tsa
Jitripatra	byi tri pa tra
Jokhang	jo khang
jungpo	'byung po
kagyé	bka' brgyad
Kagyü	bka' brgyud
kandro	mkha' 'gro
kandroma	mkha' 'gro ma
kangpé dre	khang pa'i 'dre
kangso	bskang gso
Karmashar	skar ma shar
Kham	khams
koktu zhukpa	khog tu zhugs pa
kula	sku bla
kuten	sku rten
Kyapjukchenpo	khyab 'jug chen po
Kyokchen Dangra	skyog chen sdang ra
kyung	khyung

la	bla
Lang Darma	glang dar ma
laptse	lab rtse
Lelung Jedrung Zhepé Dorjé	sle lung rje drung bzhad pa'i rdo rje
lha	lha
lhabap	lha 'bab
lhaka	lha bka'
lhalu degyé	lha klu sde brgyad
lhamasin degyé	lha ma srin sde brgyad
lhamayin	lha ma yin
lhamin	lha min
Lhamo Lhatso	lha mo lha mtsho
lhandre	lha 'dre
lhané	lha nad
lhanyen	lha gnyan
lhapa	lha pa
lhasin degyé	lha srin sde brgyad
Lhodrak Kharchu	lho brag mkhar chu
Longdöl Ngawang Lozang	klong rdol ngag dbang blo bzang
losar	lo gsar
lu	klu
Lubuk	klu sbug
lugong gyelpo	glud 'gong rgyal po
lunyen	klu gnyan
luröl	klu rol
lusi	klu sri
lütor	glud gtor
Machen Pomra	rma chen spom ra
malha	ma lha
mamo	ma mo

masang püngu	ma sangs spun dgu
melong	me long
men	sman
Mentsikhang	sman rtsis khang
Meru Sarpa	rme ru gsar pa
miamchi	mi'am ci
mo	mo
mönlam chenmo	smon lam chen mo
mönpa	mon pa
mosi	mo sri
mu	dmu
namtsen	gnam btsan
Nechung	gnas chung
ngakpa	sngags pa
nöjin	gnod sbyin
Nyangrel Nyima Özer	myang ral nyi ma 'od zer
nyen	gnyan
nyenchen dezhi	gnyan chen sde bzhi
Nyenchen Tanglha	gnyan chen thang lha
Nyima Zhönnu	nyi ma gzhon nu
Nyingma	rnying ma
Odé Gungyel	'o lde gung rgyal
Ogyan Lingpa	o rgyan gling pa
parka degyé	spar kha sde brgyad
pamo	dpa' mo
pawo	dpa' bo
Pehar	pe har
Penden Lhamo	dpal ldan lha mo
penlhé ridra	dpal lha'i ri gra
polha	pho lha

posi	pho sri
purbu	phur bu
Rāhula	rA hu la
Rebkong	reb gong
rolang	ro langs
sadak	sa bdag
Sakya	sa skya
Sakya Witches	sa skya 'bag mo
Samyé	bsam yas
Sangyé Gyatso	sangs rgyas rgya mtsho
sanyen	sa gnyan
senmo	bsen mo
sétsen	sa'i btsan
Sharkok	shar khog
shaza	sha za
shédre	gshed 'dre
Shenrap Miwo	gshen rab mi bo
shidre	shi 'dre
shinjé	gshin rje
si	sri
sinpo	srin po
sipaho	srid pa ho
sokdak	srog bdag
soklha	srog lha
Sönam	bsod nams
söndre	gson 'dre
Songtsen Gampo	srong btsan sgam po
sungma	srung ma
tangka	thang ka

Tashi Lhünpo	bkra shis lhun po
tendrel	rten 'brel
Tengyeling	bstan rgyas gling
tensung marnak	bstan srung dmar nag
teurang	the'u rang
Third Tukwan Lozang Chökyi Nyima	thu'u bkwan 03 blo bzang chos kyi nyi ma
toché	lto 'phye(d)
tochechenpo	lto 'phyed chen po
torma	gtor ma
trinlé namzhi	'phrin las rnam bzhi
trülbum	grul bum
tsadak	rtsa bdag
Tsang	gtsang
Tsangpa	tshangs pa
Tsechokling	tshe mchog gling
Tsel Gungtang	tshal gung thang
tsen	btsan
tsensi	btsan sri
Tsiu Marpo	rtsi'u dmar po
Tsongkhapa Lozang Drakpa	tsong kha pa blo bzang grags pa
tsonyen	mtsho gnyan
tsünlha	mtshun lha
Twelve Tenma Goddesses	brtan ma bcu gnyis
Warlord of Yigyel	dbyi rgyal dmag dpon
Wencheng	rgya bza' kong jo
werma	wer ma
White Beryl	*baidūrya dkar po*
Yala Dendruk	ya bla bdal drug
yang	g.yang

Yarlha Shampo	yar lha sham po
yatsen	g.ya' btsan
yengjé	g.yeng byed
yidak	yi dwags
yidam	yi dam
yülha	yul lha
za	gza'
zachen gyé	gza' chen brgyad
zadre	za 'dre
zamling chisang	'dzam gling spyi bsangs
zhanglha	zhang lha
zhidak	gzhi bdag
zhing sadak	zhing sa bdag

Bibliography

Primary Sources

Bla brang skal bzang. 1996. *Bod skyong srung ma khag gi lo rgyus*. Dharamsala: H. P.

Blo bzang chos kyi nyi ma, Thu'u bkwan 03 (1737–1802). 1969–1971. *Glud gtor gyi cho ga kun phan 'dod 'jo dang / rgyal rdzong lag tu blang bde ba. In Collected Works of Thu'u-Bkwan Blo-Bzang-Chos-Kyi-Nyi-Ma*, vol.5. Gadan Sungrab Minyam Gyunphel Series, vol. V. Ngawang Gelek Demo, ed. New Delhi: Ngawang Gelek Demo, pp. 127–137.

Blo bzang dpal ldan, Dze smad. 1973. *Mthu dang stobs kyis che ba'i bstan srung chen po rdo rje shugs ldan rtsal gyi byung ba brjod pa pha rgod bla ma'i zhal gyi bdud rtsi'i chu khur brtsegs shing 'jigs rung glog zhags 'gyu ba'i sprin nag 'khrugs pa'i nga ro*. Delhi: n.p.

Blo gros mtha' yas, Kong sprul (1813–1899). 1976. *Rin chen gter mdzod chen mo: a reproduction of the Stod-lun Mtshur-phu redaction of 'Jam-mgon Kon-sprul's great work on the unity of the gter-ma traditions of Tibet, with supplemental texts from the Dpal-spuns redaction and other manuscripts*, vols. 59–63. Paro: Ngodrup and Sherab Drimay.

Bstan 'dzin rgya mtsho, ed. n.d. *Snga 'gyur rgyud 'bum las btus pa'i gtam rgyud phyogs bsgrigs*. Gser rta: gser rta dgon po'i par khang.

Bzhad pa'i rdo rje, Sle lung rje drung (1697–1740). 1976. *Dam can bstan srung rgya mtsho'i rnam par thar pa cha shas tsam brjod pa sngon med legs bshad*. Thimphu: Kunzang Topgey.

1978. *Dam can bstan srung rgya mtsho'i rnam par thar pa cha shas tsam brjod pa sngon med legs bshad*, 2 vols. Paro: Ngodrup and Sherab Drimay.

1979. *Dam can bstan srung rgya mtsho'i rnam par thar pa cha shas tsam brjod pa sngon med legs bshad*, 2 vols. Smanrtsis Shesrig Spedzod, vol. 105. Leh: T. S. Tashigang.

2003. *Dam can bstan srung gi rnam thar* [=*Dam can bstan srung rgya mtsho'i rnam par thar pa cha shas tsam brjod pa sngon med legs bshad*]. Beijing: Mi rigs dpe skrun khang.

Chandra, Lokesh, ed. 1961. *The Samye Monastery*. Bhoṭa-Piṭaka 6. New Delhi: International Academy of Indian Culture.

Dbang phyug rgyal po, Gung Bshad sgra ba. 2000. *Bsam yas dkar chag dad pa'i sgo 'byed*. Gangs can rig mdzod 34. Lhasa: Bod ljongs bod yig dpe rnying dpe skrun khang.

Dhongthog, Tenpai Gyaltsan. 1996. *The Earth Shaking Thunder of True Word: A Refutation of Attacks on the Advice of H. H. the Dalai Lama Regarding the Propitiation of Guardian Deities*. Shoreline: Shotech Press.

Mchog gyur gling pa (1829–1870). 1976. *Gsol 'debs bar chad lam sel*. In *Rin chen gter mdzod chen mo: a reproduction of the Stod-luṅ Mtshur-phu redaction of 'Jam-mgon Koṅ-sprul's great work on the unity of the gter-ma traditions of Tibet, with supplemental texts from the Dpal-spuṅs redaction and other manuscripts*, vol. 15. Paro: Ngodrup and Sherab Drimay, pp. 51–58.

Ngag dbang blo bzang, Klong rdol. 1991. *Bstan srung dam can rgya mtsho'i mtshan tho*. In *Klong rdol ngag dbang blo bzang gi gsung 'bum*, vol. 2. Lhasa: Bod ljongs bod yig dpe rnying dpe skrun khang, pp. 461–493.

Ngag dbang rgyal po, Legs bshad thogs med, and Zla ba rgyal mtshan. 2005. *Dpal bsam yas mi 'gyur lhun gyis grub pa'i gtsug lag khang gi dkar chag*. Beijing: Mi rigs dpe skrun khang.

O rgyan gling pa (1323–1360). 1996. *Padma bka' thang*. Chengdu: Si khron mi rigs dpe skrun khang.

[1986] 1997. *Bka' thang sde lnga*. Beijing: Mi rigs dpe skrun khang.

Sangs rgyas rgya mtsho, Sde srid (1653–1705). 1972. *The Vaidūrya Dkar Po of Sde-srid Saṅs-rgyas-rgya-mtsho: The Fundamental Treatise on Tibetan Astrology and Calendrical Calculations*, vol. 2. New Delhi: T. Tsepal Taikhang.

1973. *Bai Ḍūr Sṅon Po: Being the Text of the "Gso ba rig pa'i bstan bcos sman bla'i dgons rgyan rgyud bźi'i gsal byed bai ḍūr sṅon po'i ma lli ka," Sde-srid Saṅs-rgyas-rgya-mtsho's detailed synthetic treatise on the Rgyud bźi, the fundamental exposition of Tibetan ayurvedic medicine.* Smanrtsis Shesrig Spendzod, vol. 53. Leh: S.W. Tashigangpa.

Yon tan mgon po, G.yu thog (1126–1202). 1982. *Bdud rtsi snying po yan lag brgyad pa gsang ba man ngag gi rgyud.* Lhasa: Bod ljongs mi dmangs dpe skrun khang.

Secondary Sources

Achard, Jean-Luc, ed. 2002. *Revue d'Etudes Tibétaines 2: Numéro Spécial Lha srin sde brgyad.* Paris: Langues et Cultures de l'Aire Tibétaine.

2003. "Contribution aux nombrables de la tradition Bon po: *L'Appendice* de bsTan 'dzin Rin chen rgyal mtshan à la *Sphère de Cristal des Dieux et des Démons* de Shar rdza rin po che." In *Revue d'Etudes Tibétaines* 4, pp. 78–146.

Acharya, Chowang and Sonam Gyatso Dokham. 1998. "Sikkim: The Hidden Holy Land and Its Sacred Lakes." In *Bulletin of Tibetology* 34(3), pp. 10–15.

Arnott, W. Geoffrey. 1989. "Nechung: A Modern Parallel to the Delphic Oracle?" In *Greece & Rome* 36 (2), pp. 152–157.

Bailey, Cameron. 2012. "The Raven and the Serpent: 'The Great All-Pervading Rāhula' and Dæmonic Buddhism in India and Tibet." Master's thesis, Florida State University.

2017. "A Feast for Scholars: The Life and Works of Sle lung Bzhad pa'i rdo rje." Doctoral dissertation, University of Oxford.

2019a. "*The Demon Crowned with a Raven Head*: Rāhula's Archaic Form 'Ki kang' and his Chinese Origins." In *International Journal of Buddhist Thought & Culture* 29(1), pp. 149–176.

2019b. "*The Progenitor of all Dharma Protectors*: Buddhist Śaivism in Lelung Zhepe Dorje's *Ocean of Oath-Bound Protectors.*" In *Bojo Sasang* 54, pp. 180–237.

Barnett, Robert. 2012. "Notes on Contemporary Ransom Rituals in Lhasa." In *Revisiting Rituals in a Changing Tibetan World*. Katia Buffetrille, ed. Leiden: Brill, pp. 273–374.

Beer, Robert. 2004. *The Encyclopedia of Tibetan Symbols and Motifs*. Chicago: Serindia Publications.

Bell, Christopher. 2006. "Tsiu Marpo: The Career of a Tibetan Protector Deity." Master's thesis, Florida State University.

2013. "Nechung: The Ritual History and Institutionalization of a Tibetan Buddhist Protector Deity." Doctoral dissertation, University of Virginia.

2017. "The Mythic Murals of Meru Sarpa." In *Orientations* 48(1), pp. 44–52.

Bellezza, John Vincent. 1997. *Divine Dyads: Ancient Civilization in Tibet*. Dharamsala: Library of Tibetan Works and Archives.

2005. *Spirit-Mediums, Sacred Mountains and Related Bon Textual Traditions in Upper Tibet: Calling Down the Gods*. Leiden: Brill.

2008. *Zhang Zhung: Foundations of Civilization in Tibet. A Historical and Ethnoarchaeological Study of the Monuments, Rock Art, Texts, and Oral Tradition of the Ancient Tibetan Upland*. Vienna: Verlag der Österreichischen Akademie der Wissenschaften.

2010. "gShen-rab Myi-bo: His Life and Times According to Tibet's Earliest Literary Sources." In *Revue d'Etudes Tibétaines* 19, pp. 31–118.

2011. "The Liturgies and Oracular Utterances of the Spirit-mediums of Upper Tibet: An Introduction to their *bSang* Rituals." In *Revue d'Etudes Tibétaines* 20, pp. 5–31.

Bentor, Yael. 1996. *Consecration of Images and Stūpas in Indo-Tibetan Tantric Buddhism*. Leiden: E. J. Brill.

Berglie, Per-Arne. 1976. "Preliminary Remarks on Some Tibetan 'Spirit Mediums' in Nepal." In *Kailash* 4(1), pp. 85–108.

1992. "Tibetan Spirit-Mediumship: Change and Continuity. Some Observations from a Revisit to Nepal." In *Tibetan Studies: Proceedings of the Fifth Seminar of the International Association for Tibetan Studies, Narita 1989*, vol. 2. Ihara Shōren and Yamaguchi Zuihō, eds. Tokyo: Naritasan Shinshoji, pp. 361–368.

Berounský, Daniel. 2007. "Iconography and Texts of the Tibetan Five Protecting Deities." In *Filosofiya, Religiya i Kul'tura stran Vostoka: Materialy Nauchnoi Konferencii, 7–10 October 2007*. S. V. Pakhomov, ed. Saint Petersburg: Izdatelstvo Sankt Petergburgskogo Universitěta, pp. 331–340.

2008. "Powerful Hero *(Dpa' rtsal)*: Protective Deity from the 19th Century Amdo and his Mediums." In *Mongolo-Tibetica Pragensia '08. Special Issue: Mediums and Shamans in Central Asia*, vol. 1(2). Daniel Berounský, ed. Prague: Triton, pp. 67–115.

2009. "'Soul of Enemy' and Warrior Deities *(dgra bla)*: Two Tibetan Myths on Primordial Battle." In *Mongolo-Tibetica Pragensia '09: Ethnolinguistics, Sociolinguistics, Religion and Culture*, vol. 2(2). Jaroslav Vacek and Alena Oberfalzerová, eds. Prague: Triton, pp. 19–57.

2010. "Opice a Démon Theurang: Tibetské Mýty a Ochranné Obrázky z Amda." In *Zvířecí Mýty a Myticka Zvířata*. Lucie Olivová, ed. Prague: Academia Praha, pp. 28–47.

2012. "The Murdered King Protecting Fields: A Tibetan Deity-Medium from the Bonpo Village in Amdo." In *Mongolo-Tibetica Pragensia '12: Ethnolinguistics, Sociolinguistics, Religion and Culture*, vol. 5(2). Jaroslav Vacek and Alena Oberfalzerová, eds. Prague: Triton, pp. 21–50.

2014. "Tibetan Myths on 'Good Fortune' *(phya)* and 'Well-being' *(g.yang)*." In *Mongolo-Tibetica Pragensia '14: Ethnolinguistics, Sociolinguistics, Religion and Culture* 7(2). Daniel Berounský, ed. Prague: Charles University in Prague Faculty of Arts, Institute of South and Central Asia Seminar of Mongolian and Tibetan Studies, pp. 55–77.

Bethlenfalvy, Géza. 2003. "Fearsome and Protective Deities; Sky-, Air-, Earth-, Mountain-, Water-Divinities; Harmful and Helpful Demons; Spirits, Ghosts, Devils and Witches in Tibet and Mongolia." In *Demons and Protectors: Folk Religion in Tibetan and Mongolian Buddhism*. Béla Kelényi, ed. Budapest: Ferenc Hopp Museum of Eastern Asiatic Art, pp. 27–46.

Beyer, Stephan. 1978. *The Cult of Tara: Magic and Ritual in Tibet*. Berkeley: University of California Press.

Bhattacharyya, N. N. 2000. *Indian Demonology: The Inverted Pantheon*. New Delhi: Manohar.

Blezer, Henk. 2004. "The 'Bon' *dBal-mo Nyer-bdun (/brgyad)* and the Buddhist *dBang-phyug-ma Nyer-brgyad*: A Brief Comparison." In *New Horizons in Bon Studies*. Samten G. Karmay and Yasuhiko Nagano, eds. Delhi: Saujanya Publications, pp. 117–178.

Blondeau, Anne-Marie. 1971. "Le Lha 'dre bka'-thaṅ." In *Études Tibétaines Dédiées à la Mémoire de Marcelle Lalou*. Adrien Maisonneuve, ed. Paris: Librairie d'Amérique et d'Orient, pp. 29–126.

1976. "Les Religions du Tibet." In *Histoire des Religions, Encyclopédie de la Pléiade*, vol.3. Henri-Charles Puech, ed. Paris: Gallimard, pp. 233–249.

1990. "Questions Préliminaires sur les Rituels *mdos*." In *Tibet: Civilisation et Société*. Fernand Meyer, ed. Paris: Éditions de la Fondation Singer-Polignac, pp. 91–107.

ed. 1998. *Tibetan Mountain Deities, Their Cults and Representations*. Vienna: Verlag der Österreichischen Akademie Der Wissenschaften.

2002. "Les *Ma mo*: Mythes Cosmogoniques et Théogoniques dans le *rNying ma'i rgyud 'bum*." In *The Many Canons of Tibetan Buddhism: PIATS 2000: Tibetan Studies: Proceedings of the Ninth Seminar of the International Association for Tibetan Studies, Leiden 2000*. Helmut Eimer and David Germano, eds. Leiden: Brill, pp. 293–311.

2004. "The *mKha' klong gsang mdos*: Some Questions on Ritual Structure and Cosmology," In *New Horizons in Bon Studies*. Samten Karmay and Yasuhiko Nagano, eds. Delhi: Saujanya Publications, pp. 249–287.

2008. "Le Réseau des Mille Dieux et Démons: Mythes et Classifications." In *Revue d'Etudes Tibétaines* 15, pp. 199–250.

Blondeau, Anne-Marie, and Ernst Steinkellner, eds. 1996. *Reflections of the Mountain: Essays on the History and Social Meaning of the Mountain Cult in Tibet and the Himalaya*. Vienna: Verlag der Österreichischen Akademie der Wissenschaften.

Buffetrille, Katia. 2002. "Qui est Khri ka'i yul lha? Dieu Tibétain du Terroir, Dieu Chinois de la Littérature ou de la Guerre? Un Problème d'Identité Divine en A mdo." In *Territory and Identity in Tibet and the Himalayas: PIATS 2000: Tibetan Studies: Proceedings of the Ninth Seminar of the International Association for Tibetan Studies, Leiden 2000*. Katia Buffetrille and Hildegard Diemberger, eds. Leiden: Brill, pp. 135–155.

Cabezón, José, ed. 2010. *Tibetan Ritual*. Oxford: Oxford University Press.

Cantwell, Catherine. 1997. "To Meditate upon Consciousness as Vajra: Ritual 'Killing and Liberation' in the Rnying-ma-pa Tradition." In *Tibetan Studies: Proceedings of the Seventh Seminar of the International Association for Tibetan Studies, Graz 1995*. Helmut Eimer, ed. Vienna: Verlag der Österreichischen Akademie der Wissenschaften, pp. 107–118.

2005. "The Earth Ritual: Subjugation and Transformation of the Environment." In *Revue d'Etudes Tibétaines* 7, pp. 4–21.

Cantwell, Catherine and Robert Mayer. 2013. "Representations of Padmasambhava in Early Post-Imperial Tibet." In *Tibet after Empire: Culture, Society and Religion between 850–1000. Proceedings of the Seminar Held in Lumbini, Nepal, March 2011*. Christoph Cüppers, Robert Mayer, and Michael Walter, eds. Lumbini: Lumbini International Research Institute, pp. 19–50.

Central Tibetan Secretariat Information Office, Tsering Tashi, and Tsepak Rinzin. 1992. "Nechung: The State Oracle of Tibet." In *Tibetan Bulletin*, July/August, pp. 16–32.

Chabpel Tseten Phuntsok. 1991. "The Deity Invocation Ritual and the Purification Rite of Incense Burning in Tibet." Thubten K. Rikey, trans. In *The Tibet Journal* 16(3), pp. 3–27.

Chandra, Lokesh and Fredrick W. Bunce. 2002. *The Tibetan Iconography of Buddhas, Bodhisattvas and Other Deities: A Unique Pantheon*. New Delhi: D. K. Printworld.

Chandra, Raghu Vira and Lokesh Chandra, eds. 1961–1972. *A New Tibeto-Mongol Pantheon*. Śata-piṭaka Series 21. New Delhi: International Academy of Indian Culture.

Childs, Geoff. 2004. *Tibetan Diary: From Birth to Death and Beyond in a Himalayan Valley of Nepal*. Berkeley: University of California Press.

Chime Radha Rinpoche. 1981. "Tibet." In *Oracles and Divination*. Michael Loewe and Carmen Blacker, eds. Boulder: Shambhala Publications, pp. 3–37.

Conrad, Sara Marie. 2012. "Oral Accounts of the Sa skya 'bag mo, Past and Present Voices of the Terrifying Witches of Sa skya." Master's thesis, Indiana University.

Cornu, Philippe. 1990. *l'Astrologie Tibétaine*. Paris: Collection Présences. 2002. *Tibetan Astrology*. Hamish Gregor, trans. Boston: Shambhala.

Craig, Sienna. 2012. *Healing Elements: Efficacy and the Social Ecologies of Tibetan Medicine*. Berkeley: University of California Press.

Cuevas, Bryan J. 2011. "Illustrations of Human Effigies in Tibetan Ritual Texts, with Remarks on Specific Anatomical Figures and Their Possible Iconographic Source." In *Journal of the Royal Asiatic Society* (Third Series) 21(1), pp. 73–97.

2015. *The All-Pervading Melodious Drumbeat: The Life of Ra Lotsawa*. New York: Penguin.

2019. "The Politics of Magical Warfare." In *Faith and Empire: Art, Politics and Tibetan Buddhism*. Karl Debreczeny, ed. New York: Rubin Museum of Art, pp. 170–189.

Dalton, Jacob. 2004. "The Early Development of the Padmasambhava Legend in Tibet: A Study of IOL Tib J 644 and Pelliot tibétain 307." In *Journal of the American Oriental Society* 124(4), pp. 759–772.

2005. "A Crisis of Doxography: How Tibetans Organized Tantra during the 8th–12th Centuries." In the *Journal of the International Association of Buddhist Studies* 28(1), pp. 115–181.

2011. *The Taming of the Demons: Violence and Liberation in Tibetan Buddhism*. New Haven: Yale University Press.

2016. *The Gathering of Intentions: A History of a Tibetan Tantra*. New York: Columbia University Press.

Danzang Cairang. 2009. "The 'Spirit Mediums' (*Lha pa*) of Reb gong in A mdo." In *Buddhism Beyond the Monastery: Tantric Practices and their Performers in Tibet and the Himalayas. PIATS 2003: Tibetan Studies: Proceedings of the Tenth Seminar of the International Association for Tibetan Studies, Oxford, 2003*, vol. 12. Sarah Jacoby and Antonio Terrone, eds. Leiden: Brill, pp. 163–188.

Dargyay, Eva. 1985. "The White and Red Rong-Btsan of Matho Monastery." In *Journal of the Tibet Society* 5, pp. 55–65.

1988. "Buddhism in Adaptation: Ancestor Gods and Their Tantric Counterparts in the Religious Life of Zanskar." In *History of Religions* 28(2), pp. 123–134.

Davidson, Ronald M. 2003. "Reflections on the Maheśvara subjugation myth: Indic materials, Sa-skya-pa apologetics, and the birth of Heruka." In *History of Tibet*, vol. 2. Alex McKay, ed. London: RoutledgeCurzon, pp. 206–232.

2005. *Tibetan Renaissance: Tantric Buddhism in the Rebirth of Tibetan Culture*. New York: Columbia University Press.

Day, Sophie. 1989. "Embodying Spirits: Village Oracles and Possession Ritual in Ladakh, North India." Doctoral dissertation, London School of Economics and Political Science.

1990. "Ordering Spirits: The Initiation of Village Oracles in Ladakh." In *Wissenschaftsgeschichte und gegenwärtige Forschungen in Nordwest-Indien* 9(3), pp. 206–222.

Deane, Susannah. 2014. "Sowa Rigpa, Spirits and Biomedicine: Lay Tibetan Perspectives on Mental Illness and its Healing in a Medically-pluralistic Context in Darjeeling, Northeast India." Doctoral dissertation, Cardiff University.

Decleer, Hubert. 1978. "The Working of Sādhana: Vajrabhairava." In *Tibetan Studies: Proceedings of the First Seminar of the International Association for Tibetan Studies, Zurich 1977*. Martin Brauen and Per Kvaerne, eds. Zurich: Völkerkundemuseum der Universität Zürich, pp. 113–123.

Denjongpa, Anna Balikci. 2002. "Kangchendzönga: Secular and Buddhist Perceptions of the Mountain Deity of Sikkim Among the Lhopos." In *Bulletin of Tibetology* 38(2), pp. 5–37.

Diemberger, Hildegard. 1993. "Gangla Tshechu, Beyul Khenbalung: Pilgrimage to Hidden Valleys, Sacred Mountains and Springs of Life Water in Southern Tibet and Eastern Nepal." In *Proceedings of the International Seminar on the Anthropology of Tibet and the Himalaya; September 21–28, 1990, Zurich*. Charles Ramble and Martin Brauen, eds. Druck: BuchsDruck, pp. 60–72.

2005. "Female Oracles in Modern Tibet." In *Women in Tibet*. Janet Gyatso and Hanna Havnevik, eds. New York: Columbia University Press.

2007. "Padmasambhava's Unfinished Job: The Subjugation of Local Deities as Described in the *dBa' bzhed* in Light of Contemporary Practices of Spirit Possession." In *Pramāṇakīrtiḥ: Papers Dedicated to*

Ernst Steinkellner on the Occasion of His 70th Birthday, Part 1. Birgit Kellner, Helmut Krasser, Horst Lasic, Michael Torsten Much, and Helmut Tauscher, eds. Vienna: Arbeitskreis für Tibetische und Buddhistische Studien Universität Wien, pp. 85–93.

Diemberger, Hildegard and Guntram Hazod. 1997. "Animal Sacrifices and Mountain Deities in Southern Tibet." In *Les Habitants du Toit du Monde: Études Recueillies en Hommage à Alexander W. Macdonald*. Samten Karmay and Philippe Sagant, eds. Recherches sur la Haute Asie 12. Nanterre: Société d'Ethnologie, pp. 261–281.

Dobis Tsering Gyal. 2009. "Gzhung sa dga' ldan pho brang chen po'i gzhung bsten chos skyong khag la dpyad pa". In *Contemporary Visions in Tibetan Studies: Proceedings of the First International Seminar of Young Tibetologists*. Brandon Dotson, Kalsang Norbu Gurung, Georgios Halkias, and Tim Myatt, eds. Chicago: Serindia Publications, pp. 343–361.

Dorje, Gyurme. 2004. *Footprint Tibet*. 3rd ed. Bath: Footprint Travel Guides.

Dotson, Brandon. 2007. "Divination and Law in the Tibetan Empire: The Role of Dice in the Legislation of Loans, Interest, Marital Law and Troop Conscription." In *Contributions to the Cultural History of Early Tibet*. Matthew Kapstein and Brandon Dotson, eds. Leiden: Brill, pp. 3–77.

2012. "At the Behest of the Mountain: Gods, Clans and Political Topography in Post-Imperial Tibet." In *Old Tibetan Studies Dedicated to the Memory of Professor Ronald E. Emmerick (1937–2001). PIATS 2003: Tibetan Studies: Proceedings of the Tenth Seminar of the International Association for Tibetan Studies, Oxford, 2003*. Cristina A. Scherrer-Schaub, ed. Leiden: Brill, pp. 157–202.

2015. "The Call of the Cuckoo to the Thin Sheep of Spring: Healing and Fortune in Old Tibetan Dice Divination Texts." In *Tibetan and Himalayan Healing: An Anthology for Anthony Aris*. Charles Ramble and Ulrike Roesler, eds. Kathmandu: Vajra Publications, pp. 148–160.

2017. "On 'Personal Protective Deities' (*'go ba'i lha*) and the Old Tibetan Verb *'go*." In *Bulletin of the School of Oriental and African Studies* 80(3), pp. 525–545.

2018. "Divination and Buddhism in Tibet." *2018 Khyentse Lecture*. Center for Buddhist Studies, University of California, Berkeley, CA, August 2, 2018. www.youtube.com/watch?v=GTNpvPMOgCE&-feature=youtu.be

Douglas, Kenneth and Gwendolyn Bays, trans. 1978. *The Life and Liberation of Padmasambhava*, 2 vols. Berkeley: Dharma Publishing.

Dowman, Keith. 1988. *The Power-Places of Central Tibet: The Pilgrim's Guide*. London: Routledge and Kegan Paul.

Dpal-ldan-bkra-shis and Kevin Stuart. 1998. "Perilous Novelties: The A-mdo Tibetan *klu-rol* Festival in Gling-rgyal Village." In *Anthropos* 93, pp. 31–53.

Dreyfus, Georges. 1998. "The Shuk-den Affair: History and Nature of a Quarrel." In *Journal of the International Association of Buddhist Studies* 21(2), pp. 227–270.

Ehrhard, Franz-Karl. 2003. "Political and Ritual Aspects of the Search for Himalayan Sacred Lands." In *History of Tibet*, vol. 2. Alex McKay, ed. London: RoutledgeCurzon, pp. 659–674.

Ekvall, Robert. 1963. "Some Aspects of Divination in Tibetan Society." In *Ethnology* 2(1), pp. 31–39.

Farkas, János, and Tibor Szabó. 2002. *Die Bilderwelt der tibetisch-mongolischen Dämonen; The Pictorial World of the Tibeto-Mongolian Demons*. Budapest: Mandala & LibroTrade.

Faure, Bernard. 2016. *Gods of Medieval Japan, Volume 1: The Fluid Pantheon*. Honolulu: University of Hawai'i Press.

FitzHerbert, Solomon George. 2015. "On the Tibetan Ge-sar Epic in the Late 18th Century: Sum-pa mkhan-po's Letters to the 6th Paṇ-chen Lama." In *Études Mongoles et Sibériennes, Centrasiatiques et Tibétaines* 46. https://journals.openedition.org/emscat/2602.

Forgues, Grégory. 2017. "Invoquer le *Dgra lha*. Rituels Propitiatoires Adressés à Gesar dans la Tradition *Ris med* du XIXe siècle: Vue d'Ensemble et Étude de Cas." In *Musique et Épopée en Haute-Asie: Mélanges offerts à Mireille Helffer à l'Occasion de Son 90e Anniversaire*. Katia Buffetrille and Isabelle Henrion-Dourcy, eds. Paris: l'Asiathèque Maison des Langues du Monde, pp. 151–169.

Francke, A. H. 1930. "gZer Myig, i.e. Rays from the Eyes of the Svastika, a Precious Summary of the World. Book VI. Translated from the Tibetan." In *Asia Major*, (New Series) vol. 5, pp. 1–40.

Frankfurter, David. 2012. "Introduction." In *Archiv für Religionsgeschichte* 14, pp. 1–8.

Gentry, James. 2010. "Representations of Efficacy: The Ritual Expulsion of Mongol Armies in the Consolidation and Expansion of the Tsang (Gtsang) Dynasty." In *Tibetan Ritual*. José Ignacio Cabezón, ed. Oxford: Oxford University Press, pp. 131–163.

2017. *Power Objects in Tibetan Buddhism: The Life, Writings, and Legacy of Sokdokpa Lodrö Gyeltsen*. Leiden: Brill.

Gerke, Barbara. 2007. "Engaging the Subtle Body: Re-Approaching *bla* Rituals in the Himalayas," In *Soundings in Tibetan Medicine; Anthropological and Historical Perspectives: PIATS 2003: Tibetan Studies: Proceedings of the Tenth Seminar of the International Association for Tibetan Studies, Oxford, 2003*. Mona Schrempf, ed. Leiden: Brill, pp. 193–214.

Germano, David and Janet Gyatso. 2000. "Longchenpa and the Possession of the Ḍākinīs." In *Tantra in Practice*. Princeton Readings in Religions Series. David Gordon White, ed. Princeton: Princeton University Press, pp. 241–265.

Germano, David and Nicolas Tournadre. 2003. "THL Simplified Phonetic Transcription of Standard Tibetan." In *The Tibetan and Himalayan Library*. www.thlib.org/reference/transliteration/#!essay=/thl/phonetics/.

Getty, Alice. [1914] 1962. *The Gods of Northern Buddhism: Their History, Iconography and Progressive Evolution through the Northern Buddhist Countries*. Rutland: Charles E. Tuttle Company.

Gibson, Todd Allen. 1985. "Dgra-lha: A Re-Examination." In *Journal of the Tibet Society* 5, pp. 67–72.

    1991. "From *btsanpo* to *btsan*: The Demonization of the Tibetan Sacral Kingship." Doctoral dissertation, Indiana University.

Grenet, Franz. 2000. "Avatars de Vaiśravaṇa: les Étapes Sogdienne et Tibétaine," In *La Sérinde, Terre d'Échanges: Art, Religion, Commerce du Ier au Xe Siècle*. Monique Cohen, Jean-Pierre Drège, and Jacques Giès, eds. Paris: La Documentation Française, pp. 169–179.

Grizman, Guy. 2016. "The Sādhanic Sector: Narratives on the Origination and Transmission of the bKa'-brgyad Cycle of Tantric Teachings in India and Tibet." Paper presented at the 14th Seminar of the International Association for Tibetan Studies, Bergen, Norway. Unpublished.

Guidoni, Rachel. 1998. "l'Ancienne Cérémonie d'État du Glud.'gong rgyal.po à Lhasa." Master's thesis, Université Paris Ouest Nanterre La Défense.

Gutschow, Niels, and Charles Ramble. 2003. "Up and Down, Inside and Outside: Notions of Space and Territory in Tibetan Villages of Mustang, Nepal." In *Sacred Landscape in the Himalaya*. Niels Gutschow, Axel Michaels, Charles Ramble, and Ernst Steinkellner, eds. Vienna: Verlag der Österreichischen Akademie der Wissenschaften, pp. 137–176.

Gyaltsen, Sakyapa Sonam. 1996. *The Clear Mirror: A Traditional Account of Tibet's Golden Age*. Ithaca: Snow Lion Publications.

Gyatso, Janet. 1987. "Down with the Demoness: Reflections on a Feminine Ground in Tibet." In *The Tibet Journal* 12(4), pp. 38–53.

    1997. "An Avalokiteśvara Sādhana." In *Religions of Tibet in Practice*. Princeton Readings in Religions. Donald S. Lopez, Jr., ed. Princeton: Princeton University Press, pp. 266–270.

2015. *Being Human in a Buddhist World: An Intellectual History of Medicine in Early Modern Tibet*. New York: Columbia University Press.

G.yung 'brug and Rin chen rdo rje. 2011. "Dmu rdo: A Powerful Hero and Mountain Deity." In *Asian Highlands Perspectives* 10, pp. 73–98.

Haarh, Erik. 1969. *The Yar-luṅ Dynasty*. Copenhagen: G. E. C. Gad's Forlag.

Hao, Wangdui and Xiao Hao. 1992. "Between God and Human Beings: A Visit to Sorceress Losang Zizen." In *China's Tibet* 3(1), pp. 32–40.

Harper, Donald. 1985. "A Chinese Demonography of the Third Century BC." In *Harvard Journal of Asiatic Studies* 45(2), pp. 459–498.

Havnevik, Hanna. 2002. "A Tibetan Female State Oracle." In *Religion and Secular Culture in Tibet; Tibetan Studies: Proceedings of the Ninth Seminar of the International Association for Tibetan Studies*, Leiden 2000. Henk Blezer, ed. Leiden: Brill, pp. 259–287.

Heller, Amy. 1985. "An Early Tibetan Ritual: Rkyal 'bud." In *Soundings in Tibetan Civilization*. Barbara Aziz and Matthew Kapstein, eds. New Delhi: Manohar Publications, pp. 257–267.

1988. "Early Textual Sources for the Cult of Beg-ce." In *Tibetan Studies: Proceedings of the 4th Seminar of the International Association for Tibetan Studies. Schloss Hohenkammer – Munich 1985*. Helga Uebach and Jampa L. Panglung, eds. Munich: Kommission für Zentralasiatische Studien Bayerische Akademie der Wissenschaften, pp. 185–195.

1990. "Remarques Préliminaires sur les Divinités Protectrices Srung-ma dmar-nag du Potala." In *Tibet, Civilisation et Société*. Paris: Éditions de la Maison des Sciences de l'Homme, pp. 19–27 and plates.

1992a. "Historic and Iconographic Aspects of the Protective Deities Srung-ma dmar-nag." In *Tibetan Studies: Proceedings of the 5th Seminar of the International Association for Tibetan Studies, Narita 1989*, vol 2. Ihara Shōren and Yamaguchi Zuihō, eds. Tokyo: Naritasan Shinshoji, pp. 479–492.

1992b. "Etude sur le développement de l'iconographie et du culte de Begtse, divinité protectrice tibétaine." Paris: Diplôme de l'École Pratique
des Hautes Études.

1996. "Mongolian Mountain Deities and Local Gods: Examples of Rituals
for their Worship in Tibetan Language." In *Reflections of the Mountain:
Essays on the History and Social Meaning of the Mountain Cult in Tibet and
the Himalaya.* Anne-Marie Blondeau and Ernst Steinkellner, eds. Vienna:
Verlag der Österreichischen Akademie der Wissenschaften, pp. 133–140.

1997. "Notes on the Symbol of the Scorpion in Tibet." In *Les Habitants
du Toit du Monde, Études Recueillies en Hommage à Alexander
W.* Macdonald. Samten Karmay and Philippe Sagant, eds. Nanterre:
Société d'Ethnologie, pp. 283–297.

2001. "On the Development of the Iconography of Acala and Vighnāntaka
in Tibet." In *Embodying Wisdom: Art, Text and Interpretation in the
History of Esoteric Buddhism.* Rob Linrothe and Henrik H. Sørensen,
eds. Copenhagen: Seminar for Buddhist Studies, pp. 209–228.

2003. "The Great Protector Deities of the Dalai Lamas." In *Lhasa in the
Seventeenth Century: The Capital of the Dalai Lamas.* Françoise Pommaret,
ed. Leiden: Brill, pp. 81–98.

2006. "Armor and Weapons in the Iconography of Tibetan Buddhist
Deities." In *Warriors of the Himalayas: Rediscovering the Arms and
Armor of Tibet.* Donald J. LaRocca, ed. New Haven: Yale University
Press, pp. 34–41.

Herrmann-Pfandt, Adelheid. 1992–1993. "Dakinis in Indo-Tibetan Tantric
Buddhism: Some Results of Recent Research." In *Studies in Central
and East Asian Religions* 5–6, pp. 45–63.

Hill, Nathan. 2015. "The *sku bla* Rite in Imperial Tibetan Religion." In
Cahiers d'Extrême-Asie 24, pp. 49–58.

Hirshberg, Daniel. 2016. *Remembering the Lotus-Born: Padmasambhava in
the History of Tibet's Golden Age.* Somerville: Wisdom Publications.

Huber, Toni. 1999a. *The Cult of Pure Crystal Mountain: Popular Pilgrimage and Visionary Landscape in Southeast Tibet*. New York: Oxford University Press.

ed. 1999b. *Sacred Spaces and Powerful Places in Tibetan Culture: A Collection of Essays*. Dharamsala: Library of Tibetan Works and Archives.

2013. "The Iconography of *gShen* Priests in the Ethnographic Context of the Extended Eastern Himalayas, and Reflections on the Development of Bon Religion." In *Nepalica-Tibetica: Festgabe for Christoph Cüppers*, vol. 1. Franz-Karl Ehrhard and Petra Maurer, eds. Andiast: International Institute for Tibetan and Buddhist Studies, pp. 263–294.

Hummel, Siegbert. 1962. "Pe-har." In *East and West* 13(4), pp. 313–316.

Imaeda, Yoshiro. 1973. "Une Note sur le Rite du Glud-'goṅ Rgyal-po d'Après les Sources Chinoises." In *Journal Asiatique* 266, pp. 333–339.

Jackson, Roger. 1997. "A Fasting Ritual." In *Religions of Tibet in Practice*. Princeton Readings in Religions. Donald S. Lopez, Jr., ed. Princeton: Princeton University Press, pp. 271–292.

Joffe, Ben. 2016. "Demon Directories: On Listing and Living with Tibetan Worldly Spirits." *A Perfumed Skull: Anthropology, Esotericism, and Notes on the Numinous*. Personal Blog. https://perfumedskull.com/2016/06/05/demon-directories-on-listing-and-living-with-tibetan-worldly-spirits/

Jovic, Nika. 2010. "The Cult of the 'Go ba'i lha lnga: A Study with Pictorial and Written Material of the Five Personal Protective Deities." Master's thesis, University of Vienna.

Kapstein, Matthew. 1992. "Remarks on the Maṇi Bka'-'bum and the Cult of Āvalokiteśvara in Tibet." In *Tibetan Buddhism: Reason and Revelation*. Steven Goodman and Ronald Davidson, eds. Albandy: SUNY, pp. 79–93.

1997. "The Royal Way of Supreme Compassion." In *Religions of Tibet in Practice*. Princeton Readings in Religions Series. Donald S. Lopez, Jr., ed. Princeton: Princeton University Press, pp. 69–77.

2000. *The Tibetan Assimilation of Buddhism: Conversation, Contestation, and Memory*. Oxford: Oxford University Press.

Karma Chagmed. 1982. "The Mirror of Tibetan Omens and Superstitions." Norbu Chophel, trans. In *Tibet Journal* 7(4), pp. 86–93.

Karmay, Samten G. 1988. *Secret Visions of the Fifth Dalai Lama: The Gold Manuscript in the Fournier Collection*. London: Serindia Publications.

1998a. "The Appearance of the Little Black-headed Man." In *The Arrow and the Spindle: Studies in History, Myths, Rituals and Beliefs in Tibet*. Kathmandu: Mandala Book Point, pp. 245–281.

1998b. "The Origin Myths of the First King of Tibet as Revealed in the *Can Lnga*." In *The Arrow and the Spindle: Studies in History, Myths, Rituals and Beliefs in Tibet*. Kathmandu: Mandala Book Point, pp. 282–309.

1998c. "The Soul and the Turquoise: a Ritual for Recalling the *bla*." In *The Arrow and the Spindle: Studies in History, Myths, Rituals and Beliefs in Tibet*. Kathmandu: Mandala Book Point, pp. 310–338.

1998d. "The Man and the Ox: A Ritual for Offering the *glud*." In *The Arrow and the Spindle: Studies in History, Myths, Rituals and Beliefs in Tibet*. Kathmandu: Mandala Book Point, pp. 339–379.

1998e. "The Local Deities and the Juniper Tree: a Ritual for Purification (*bsang*)." In *The Arrow and the Spindle: Studies in History, Myths, Rituals and Beliefs in Tibet*. Kathmandu: Mandala Book Point, pp. 380–412.

1998f. "The Wind-horse and the Well-being of Man." In *The Arrow and the Spindle: Studies in History, Myths, Rituals and Beliefs in Tibet*. Kathmandu: Mandala Book Point, pp. 413–422.

1998g. "Mountain Cult and National Identity." In *The Arrow and the Spindle: Studies in History, Myths, Rituals and Beliefs in Tibet*. Kathmandu: Mandala Book Point, pp. 423–431.

1998h. "The Cult of Mountain Deities and its Political Significance." In *The Arrow and the Spindle: Studies in History, Myths, Rituals and Beliefs in Tibet*. Kathmandu: Mandala Book Point, pp. 432–450.

1998i. "The Cult of Mount dMu-rdo in rGyal-rong." In *The Arrow and the Spindle: Studies in History, Myths, Rituals and Beliefs in Tibet.* Kathmandu: Mandala Book Point, pp. 451–462.

2003. "Une note sur l'origine du concept des huit catégories d'esprits." In *Revue d'Etudes Tibétaines* 2, pp. 67–80.

2004. "A Comparative Study of the *yul lha* Cult in Two Areas and its Cosmological Aspects." In *New Horizons in Bon Studies.* Samten G. Karmay and Yasuhiko Nagano, eds. Delhi: Saujanya Publications, pp. 383–413.

2010. "Tibetan Indigenous Myths and Rituals with Reference to the Ancient Bön Text: The *Nyenbum (Gnyan'bum),*" In *Tibetan Ritual.* José Cabezón, ed. Oxford: Oxford University Press, pp. 53–68.

Kelényi, Béla, ed. 2003. *Demons and Protectors: Folk Religion in Tibetan and Mongolian Buddhism.* Budapest: Ferenc Hopp Museum of Eastern Asiatic Art.

2012. "The Representation of Astrological Knowledge in the Cult of the Tibetan Prayer Flag." In *Figurations of Time in Asia.* Morphomata 4. Dietrich Boschung and Corinna Wessels-Mevissen, eds. Munich: Wilhelm Fink Publishing, pp. 193–203.

Kelley, Glen. 1993. *Nechung, Tsang pa, Ghadong, Youdronma: Some Research on Four Tibetan Oracles and Their Deities.* Brattleboro: Independent Study Project. School for International Training.

Kirkland, J. Russell. 1982. "The Spirit of the Mountain: Myth and State in Pre-Buddhist Tibet." In *History of Religions* 21(3), pp. 257–271.

Kohn, Richard. 1997. "An Offering of Torma." In *Religions of Tibet in Practice.* Princeton Readings in Religions. Donald S. Lopez, ed. Princeton: Princeton University Press, pp. 255–265.

2001. *Lord of the Dance: The Mani Rimdu Festival in Tibet and Nepal.* Albany: SUNY Press.

Kornman, Robin, Sangye Khandro, and Lama Chönam, trans. 2015. *The Epic of Gesar of Ling: Gesar's Magical Birth, Early Years, and Coronation as King*. Boston: Shambhala.

Kotyk, Jeffrey. 2017. "Buddhist Astrology and Astral Magic in the Tang Dynasty." Doctoral dissertation, Leiden University.

Kvaerne, Per. 1990. "A Preliminary Study of the Bonpo Deity Khro-bo Gtso-mchog Mkha'-'gying." In *Reflections on Tibetan Culture: Essays in Memory of Turrell V. Wylie*. Studies in Asian Thought and Religion 12. Lawrence Epstein and Richard Sherburne, eds. Lewiston: Edwin Mellen Press, pp. 117–125.

    1996. *The Bon Religion of Tibet: The Iconography of a Living Tradition*. Boston: Shambhala.

    2007. "Bonpo Tantric Deities," In *Bon: The Magic Word, The Indigenous Religion of Tibet*. Samten G. Karmay and Jeff Watt, eds. New York: Rubin Museum of Art, pp. 165–180.

Ladrang Kalsang. 1996. *The Guardian Deities of Tibet*. Pema Thinley, trans. Dharamsala: Little Lhasa Publications.

Laufer, Berthold. 1914. "Bird Divination among the Tibetans (Notes on Document Pelliot No.3530, with a Study of Tibetan Phonology of the Ninth Century)." In *T'oung Pao* 15, pp. 1–110.

Lin Shen-Yu. 2013. "The Fifteen Great Demons of Children." In *Revue d'Etudes Tibétaines* 26, pp. 5–33.

Lincoln, Bruce. 2012. *Gods and Demons, Priests and Scholars: Critical Explorations in the History of Religions*. Chicago: University of Chicago Press.

Linrothe, Rob and Jeff Watt. *Demonic Divine: Himalayan Art and Beyond*. Chicago: Serindia Publications.

Lohia, Sushama. 1994. *Lalitavajra's Manual of Buddhist Iconography*. Śata-Piṭaka Series: Indo-Asian Literatures, vol. 379. New Delhi: International Academy of Indian Culture and Aditya Prakashan.

Lozang Jamspal. 2006. "The Gonkhang, Temple of the Guardian Deities." In *Warriors of the Himalayas: Rediscovering the Arms and Armor of Tibet*. Donald J. LaRocca, ed. New Haven: Yale University Press, pp. 43–49.

Lucarelli, Rita. 2013. "Towards a Comparative Approach to Demonology in Antiquity: The Case of Ancient Egypt and Mesopotamia." In *Archiv für Religionsgeschichte* 14, pp. 11–25.

Macdonald, Alexander. W. 1967. *Matériaux pour l'Étude de la Littérature Populaire Tibétaine*. 2 vols. Paris: Presses Universitaires de France.

Macdonald, Ariane. 1971. "Une lecture des Pelliot Tibétain 1286, 1287, 1038, 1047, et 1290: Essai sur la formation et l'emploi des mythes politiques dans la religion royale de Sroṅ-bcan sgam-po." In *Études Tibétaines Dédiées à la Mémoire de Marcelle Lalou*. Adrien Maisonneuve, ed. Paris: Librairie d'Amérique et d'Orient, pp. 190–391.

1978a. "Le culte de Pehar et de Ci'u dmar-po dans la tradition écrite et orale. Histoire du monastère de Gnas-chung et de ses médiums (suite)," "Histoire et philologie tibétaines" (conférences 1976–1977). In *Annuaire de l'Ecole Pratique des Hautes Etudes*, Paris, pp. 1139–1145.

1978b. "Les rivalités politiques et religieuses centrées sur Samye au XVIe siècle. La lignée spirituelle du Ve Dalai-Lama dans la littérature, dans l'histoire, et dans l'art." "Histoire et philologie tibétaines" (conférences 1977–1978). In *Annuaire de l'Ecole Pratique des Hautes Etudes*, Paris, pp. 1023–1030.

Makley, Charlene. 2018. *The Battle for Fortune: State-led Development, Personhood, and Power Among Tibetans in China*. Ithaca: Cornell University Press.

Marko, Ann. 2003. "Civilising Woman the Demon: A Tibetan Myth of State." In *History of Tibet*, vol. 1. Alex McKay, ed. London: RoutledgeCurzon, pp. 322–335.

Martin, Dan. 1996a. "The Star King and the Four Children of Pehar: Popular Religious Movements of 11th-to 12th-century Tibet." In *Acta Orientalia Academiae Scientiarum Hungaricae* 49(1–2), pp. 171–195.

1996b. "Lay Religious Movements in 11th- and 12th-Century Tibet: A Survey of Sources." In *Kailash* 18(3–4), pp. 23–55.

Martin du Gard, Irène. 1971. "Génies et Démons au Tibet." In *Génies, Anges et Démons. Sources Orientales* 8. Marcel Leibovici, ed. Paris: Éditions du Seuil, pp. 383–402.

Maurer, Petra. 2009. "*Sa Bdag* and Tortoise: A Survey of the Tradition of Geomancy in Ladakh." In *Mountains, Monasteries and Mosques: Recent Research on Ladakh and the Western Himalaya. Proceedings of the 13ᵗʰ Colloquium of the International Association for Ladakh Studies*. John Bray and Elena de Rossi Filibeck, eds. Pisa: Fabrizio Serra Editore, pp. 209–219.

Maurer, Petra, Donatella Rossi, and Rolf Scheuermann, eds. 2020. *Glimpses of Tibetan Divination: Past and Present*. Leiden: Brill.

Mayer, Robert. 1996. *A Scripture of the Ancient Tantra Collection: The Phurpa bcu-gnyis*. Oxford: Kiscadale.

1998. "The Figure of Maheśvara/Rudra in the rÑiṅ-ma-pa Tantric Tradition," In *Journal of the International Association of Buddhist Studies* 21(2), pp. 271–310.

McCune, Lindsay. 2007. "Tales of Intrigue from Tibet's Holy City: The Historical Underpinnings of a Modern Buddhist Crisis." Master's thesis, Florida State University.

McGrath, William A. 2017. "Vessel Examination in the *Medicine of the Moon King*." In *Buddhism and Medicine: An Anthology of Premodern Sources*. C. Pierce Salguero, ed. New York: Columbia University Press, pp. 501–513.

Mikles, Natasha. 2016. "Buddhicizing the Warrior-King Gesar in the *dMyal gling rDzogs pa Chen po*." In *Revue d'Etudes Tibétaines* 37, pp. 231–246.

Miller, Robert. 1998. "'The Supine Demoness' (Srin mo) and the Consolidation of Empire." In *The Tibet Journal* 23(3), pp. 3–22.

Mills, Martin. 2003. *Identity, Ritual, and State in Tibetan Buddhism: The Foundations of Authority in Gelukpa Monasticism*. London: Routledge-Curzon.

    2007. "Re-Assessing the Supine Demoness: Royal Buddhist Geomancy in the Srong btsan sgam po Mythology." In *Journal of the International Association of Tibetan Studies* 3, pp. 1–47.

Mitra, Mallar. 1999. "Goddess Vajravarahi: An Iconographical Study." In *Tantric Buddhism: Centennial Tribute to Dr. Benoytosh Bhattacharyya*. N. N. Bhattacharyya and Amartya Ghosh, eds. New Delhi: Manohar, pp. 102–129.

Mori, Masahide. 2004. "The Bon Deities Depicted in the Wall Paintings in the Bon-brgya Monastery." In *New Horizons in Bon Studies*. Samten G. Karmay and Yasuhiko Nagano, eds. Delhi: Saujanya Publications, pp. 509–549.

Mortensen, Eric. 2003. "Raven Augury in Tibet, Northwest Yunnan, Inner Asia, and Circumpolar Regions." Doctoral dissertation, Harvard University.

Muldowney, Kristen. 2011. "Outward Beauty, Hidden Wrath: An Exploration of the Drikung Kagyü Dharma Protectress Achi Chökyi Drölma." Master's thesis, Florida State University.

Mumford, Stan. 1989. *Himalayan Dialogue: Tibetan Lamas and Gurung Shamans in Nepal*. Madison: University of Wisconsin Press.

Nagano, Sadako. 2004. "Sacrifice and *lha pa* in the glu rol Festival of Reb-skong." In *New Horizons in Bon Studies*. Samten G. Karmay and Yasuhiko Nagano, eds. Delhi: Saujanya Publications, pp. 567–649.

Nair, Urmila. 2004. "The Sociological Inflection of Ontology: A Study of the Multiple Ontological Statuses of a Tibetan Buddhist Protective Deity." Master's thesis, University of Chicago.

2010. "When the Sun's Rays are as Shadows: The Nechung Rituals and the Politics of Spectacle in Tibetan Exile." Doctoral dissertation, University of Chicago.

Namkhai Norbu. 1995. *Drung, Deu and Bön: Narrations, symbolic languages and the Bön tradition in ancient Tibet.* Andrew Lukianowicz, trans. Dharamsala: Library of Tibetan Works and Archives.

Narayanan, Kumar. 2003. "Between Worlds: Guardians in Tibet as Agents of Transformation." In *Perspectives* 4(3), pp. 45–62.

Nebesky-Wojkowitz, René de. 1956. *Where the Gods are Mountains.* London: Weidenfeld and Nicolson.

1976. *Tibetan Religious Dances: Tibetan Text and Annotated Translation of the 'Chams Yig.* Christoph von Fürer-Haimendorf, ed. The Hague: Mouton.

[1956] 1998. *Oracles and Demons of Tibet: The Cult and Iconography of the Tibetan Protective Deities.* New Delhi: Paljor Publications.

Nebesky-Wojkowitz, René de, and Geoffrey Gorer. 1950–1951. "The Use of Thread-Crosses in Lepcha Lamaist Ceremonies," In *The Eastern Anthropologist* 4(2), pp. 65–87.

Nielsen, Solvej. 2018. "Tibetan Buddhist Divination: The Genre and its Concepts of Fortune and Causality." Master's thesis, University of Copenhagen.

Niermann, Kristina. 2008. "Menschen und lokale Gottheiten (*lu*) im buddhistischen Ladakh: Tabus, Krankheit und Heilung im Alltag." Master's thesis, Humboldt-Universität zu Berlin.

Nishida, Ai. 2013. "Bird Divination in Old Tibetan Texts." In *Current Issues and Progress in Tibetan Studies: Proceedings of the Third International Seminar of Young Tibetologists, Kobe 2012.*" Tsuguhito Takeuchi, Kazushi Iwao, Ai Nishida, Seiji Kumagai, and Meishi Yamamoto, eds. Kobe: Kobe City University of Foreign Studies, pp. 317–341.

2016. "Old Tibetan Scapulimancy," In *Revue d'Etudes Tibétaines* 37, pp. 262–277.

Orofino, Giacomella. 1994. "Divination with Mirrors: Observations on a Simile Found in the Kālacakra Literature," In *Tibetan Studies: Proceedings of the 6th Seminar of the International Association for Tibetan Studies, Fagernes 1992*, vol. 2. Per Kvaerne, ed. Oslo: Institute for Comparative Research in Human Culture, pp. 612–628.

Parfionovitch, Yuri, Fernand Meyer, and Gyurme Dorje, eds. 1992. *Tibetan Medical Paintings: Illustrations to the* Blue Beryl *treatise of Sangye Gyatso (1653–1705)*, 2 vols. New York: Harry N. Abrams, Inc.

Penick, Douglas. 1996. *The Warrior Song of King Gesar*. Somerville: Wisdom Publications.

Peter, Prince of Greece and Denmark. 1978a. "Tibetan Oracles in Dharamsala." In *Proceedings of the Csoma de Körös Memorial Symposium*. Louis Ligeti, ed. Budapest: Akadémiai Kiadó, pp. 327–334.

    1978b. "Tibetan Oracles." In *Himalayan Anthropology: The Indo-Tibetan Interface*. Hague: Moulon, pp. 287–298.

Pommaret, Françoise. 1994. "Les Fêtes aux Divinités-Montagnes Phyva au Bhoutan de l'Est." In *Tibetan Studies: Proceedings of the 6th Seminar of the International Association for Tibetan Studies*, vol. 2. Per Kvaerne, ed. Oslo: Institute for Comparative Research in Human Culture, pp. 660–669.

    1996. "On Local and Mountain Deities in Bhutan." In *Reflections of the Mountain: Essays on the History and Social Meaning of the Mountain Cult in Tibet and the Himalaya*. Anne-Marie Blondeau and Ernst Steinkellner, eds. Vienna: Verlag der Österreichischen Akademie der Wissenschaften, pp. 39–56.

    2003a. "Etres Soumis, Etres Protecteurs: Padmasambhava et les Huit Categories de Dieux et Demons au Bhoutan." In *Revue d'Etudes Tibétaines* 2, pp. 40–66.

    ed. 2003b. *Lhasa in the Seventeenth Century: The Capital of the Dalai Lamas*. Howard Solverson, trans. Leiden: Brill.

2007. "Estate and Deities: a Ritual from Central Bhutan. The *Bskang gso* of O rgyan chos gling." In *Bhutan: Traditions and Changes. PIATS 2003: Tibetan Studies: Proceedings of the Tenth Seminar of the International Association for Tibetan Studies, Oxford, 2003*, vol. 5. John Ardussi and Françoise Pommaret, eds. Leiden: Brill, pp. 135–158.

Ramble, Charles. 1996. "Patterns of Places." In *Reflections of the Mountain: Essays on the History and Social Meaning of the Mountain Cult in Tibet and the Himalaya*. Anne-Marie Blondeau and Ernst Steinkellner, eds. Vienna: Verlag der Österreichischen Akademie der Wissenschaften, pp. 141–153.

2008. *The Navel of the Demoness: Tibetan Buddhism and Civil Religion in Highland Nepal*. Oxford: Oxford University Press.

2015. "Trouble with Vampires: Or, How the Layout of This Book Came to be Done." In *Tibetan and Himalayan Healing: An Anthology for Anthony Aris*. Charles Ramble and Ulrike Roesler, eds. Kathmandu: Vajra Books, pp. 555–570.

2017. "From 'Greatest Leaders' to 'Gnomes': The Decline of Tibetan Vampires and the Rituals for their Subjugation." Paper presented at the Deities, Spirits and Demons in Vernacular Beliefs and Rituals in Asia Conference, University of Tartu, Estonia. Unpublished.

Rangjung Yeshe Wiki. 2018. *Dharma Dictionary: Bod skad dang dbyin skad tshal mdzod thabs shes ldan pa; Tibetan-English Dictionary, Dharma Glossaries, and Resources*. http://rywiki.tsadra.org/.

Reb gong pa Mkhar rtse rgyal. 2009. *'Jig rten mchod bstod: Mdo smad reb gong yul gyi drug pa'i lha zla chen mo'i mchod pa dang 'brel ba'i dmangs srol rig gnas lo rgyus skor gyi zhib 'jug*. Beijing: Krung go'i bod rig pa dpe skrun khang.

Reinhart, Johan. 1978. "Khenbalung: The Hidden Valley." In *Kailash* 6(1), pp. 5–35.

Ricca, Franco. 1999. *Il Tempio Oracolare di Gnas-chuṅ: Gli dei del Tibet più Magico e Segreto*. Orientalia 8. Torino: Edizioni dell'Orso.

Ricca, Franco, and Lionel Fournier. 1996. "Notes Concerning the Mgon-khaṅ of Źwa-lu." In *Artibus Asiae* 56(3/4), pp. 343–363.

Richardson, Hugh. 1993. *Ceremonies of the Lhasa Year*. London: Serindia Publications.

1998. "The Cult of Vairocana in Early Tibet." In *High Peaks, Pure Earth: Collected Writings on Tibetan History and Culture*. London: Serindia Publications, pp. 177–181.

Rock, Joseph F. 1935. "Sungmas, the Living Oracles of the Tibetan Church." In *National Geographic Magazine* 68, pp. 475–486.

1959. "Contributions to the Shamanism of the Tibetan-Chinese Borderland." In *Anthropos* 54, pp. 796–818.

Ruegg, David. 2008. *The Symbiosis of Buddhism with Brahmanism/Hinduism in South Asia and of Buddhism with 'Local Cults' in Tibet and the Himalayan Region*. Vienna: Verlag der Österreichischen Akademie der Wissenschaften.

Samuel, Geoffrey. 1993. *Civilized Shamans*. Washington: Smithsonian Institution Press.

1995. "Gesar Epic of East Tibet." In *Tibetan Literature: Studies in Genre*. Jose Ignacio Cabezon, ed. Boston: Snow Lion, pp. 358–367.

2007. "Spirit Causation and Illness in Tibetan Medicine." In *Soundings in Tibetan Medicine: Anthropological and Historical Perspectives. PIATS 2003: Tibetan Studies: Proceedings of the Tenth Seminar of the International Association for Tibetan Studies, Oxford, 2003*, vol. 10. Mona Schrempf, ed. Leiden: Brill, pp. 213–224.

2010. "Healing, Efficacy and the Spirits." In *Journal of Ritual Studies* 24 (2), pp. 7–20.

2017. "Dancers in the Temple: Reflections on Tibetan Ritual and Ritual Dance." In *Musique et Épopée en Haute-Asie: Mélanges offerts à Mireille Helffer à l'Occasion de Son 90ᵉ Anniversaire*. Katia Buffetrille and Isabelle Henrion-Dourcy, eds. Paris: l'Asiathèque Maison des Langues du Monde, pp. 173–190.

Sardar-Afkhami, Abdol-Hamid. 1996. "An Account of Padma-bkod: A Hidden Land in Southeastern Tibet." In *Kailash* 18(3–4), pp. 1–21.

2001. "The Buddha's Secret Gardens: End Times and Hidden-lands in Tibetan Imagination." Doctoral dissertation, Harvard University.

Sárközi, Alice. 2012. "The Fifteen Demons Causing Child-Disease." In *Acta Orientalia Academiae Scientiarum Hungaricae* 65(2), pp. 223–234.

Schenk, Amelia. 1993. "Inducing Trance: On the Training of Ladakhi Oracle Healers." In *Proceedings of the International Seminar on the Anthropology of Tibet and the Himalaya; September 21–28, 1990, Zurich*. Charles Ramble and Martin Brauen, eds. Druck: BuchsDruck, pp. 331–342.

Schuh, Dieter. 2012. "Erdherrengeister (*sa-bdag*)." In *Tibet-Encyclopaedia*. Andiast: International Institute for Tibetan and Buddhist Studies. www.tibet-encyclopaedia.de/erdherren-sa-bdag.html

2013. "Zwischen Grossreich und Phyi-dar: Eine dunkle, kulturlose Zeit? Das Beispiel des Lehrsystems von sinotibetischen Divinationskalkulationen (*nag-rtsis*), Geomantie (*sa-dpyad*), gTo-Ritualen und Erdherrengeistern (*sa-bdag*)." In *Tibet after Empire: Culture, Society and Religion between 850–1000: Proceedings of the Seminar Held in Lumbini, Nepal, March 2011*. Christoph Cüppers, Robert Mayer, and Michael Walter, eds. Lumbini: Lumbini International Research Institute, pp. 313–342.

Sidky, Homayun. 2011. "The State Oracle of Tibet, Spirit Possession, and Shamanism." In *Numen* 58, pp. 71–99.

Sihlé, Nicolas. 2002. "*Lhachö* [*Lha mchod*] and *Hrinän* [*Sri gnon*]: The Structure and Diachrony of a Pair of Rituals (Baragaon, Northern Nepal)." In *Religion and Secular Culture in Tibet: Tibetan Studies II*. Henk Blezer, ed. Leiden: Brill, pp. 185–206.

2013. *Rituels Bouddhiques de Pouvoir et de Violence: la Figure du Tantriste Tibétain*. Belgium: Brepols.

Simmer-Brown, Judith. 2001. *Dakini's Warm Breath: The Feminine Principle in Tibetan Buddhism*. Boston: Shambhala.

Skorupski, Tadeusz. 1997. "In Praise of the Ḍākinīs." In *Les Habitants du Toit du Monde: Études Recueillies en Hommage à Alexander W. Macdonald*. Samten Karmay and Philippe Sagant, eds. Recherches sur la Haute Asie 12. Nanterre: Société d'Ethnologie, pp. 309–324.

Smith, Alexander, 2015. "Prognostic Structure and the Use of Trumps in Tibetan Pebble Divination." In *Magic, Ritual, and Witchcraft* 10(1), pp. 1–21.

Smith, Frederick M. 2006. *The Self Possessed: Deity and Spirit Possession in South Asian Literature and Civilization*. New York: Columbia University Press.

Smith, Jonathan Z. 1978. "Towards Interpreting Demonic Powers in Hellenistic and Roman Antiquity." In *Aufstieg und Niedergang der römishen Welt* II, 16(1), pp. 425–439.

Sneath, David. 2007. "Ritual Idioms and Spatial Orders: Comparing the Rites for Mongolian and Tibetan 'Local Deities'." In *The Mongolia-Tibet Interface: Opening New Research Terrains in Inner Asia. PIATS 2003: Tibetan Studies: Proceedings of the Tenth Seminar of the International Association for Tibetan Studies, Oxford, 2003*, vol. 9. Uradyn E. Bulag and Hildegard Diemberger, eds. Leiden: Brill, pp. 135–158.

Snellgrove, David. 1967. *The Nine Ways of Bon*. London: Oxford University Press.

[1987] 2002. *Indo-Tibetan Buddhism: Indian Buddhists and Their Tibetan Successors*. Boston: Shambhala.

Sobisch, Jan-Ulrich, and Solvej Nielsen. 2019. *Divining with Achi and Tārā: Comparative Remarks on Tibetan Dice and Mālā Divination: Tools, Poetry, Structures, and Ritual Dimensions*. Leiden: Brill.

Sørensen, Per. 1994. *Tibetan Buddhist Historiography: The Mirror Illuminating the Royal Genealogies. An Annotated Translation of the XIVth Century Tibetan Chronicle: rGyal-rabs gsal-ba'i me-long.* Wiesbaden: Harrassowitz Publishing.

Sørensen, Per K., Guntram Hazod, and Tsering Gyalbo. 2000. *Civilization at the Foot of Mount Sham-po: The Royal House of lHa Bug-pa-can and the History of g.Ya'-bzang.* Vienna: Verlag der Österreichischen Akademie der Wissenschaften.

———. 2005. *Thundering Falcon: An Inquiry into the History and Cult of Khra-'brug Tibet's First Buddhist Temple.* Vienna: Verlag der Österreichischen Akademie der Wissenschaften.

Stein, Rolf A. 1939. "Trente-Trois Fiches de Divination Tibetaines," In *Harvard Journal of Asiatic Studies* 4 (3/4), pp. 297–371.

———. 1959. *Recherches sur l'Épopée et le Barde du Tibet. Bibliothèque de l'Institut des Hautes Études Chinoises* 13. Paris: Presses Universitaires.

———. 1995. "La Soumission de Rudra et Autres Contes Tantriques," In *Journal Asiatique* 283(1), pp. 121–160.

Stoddard, Heather. 1997. "The Nine Brothers of the White High. Mi-nyag and 'King' Pe-dkar Revisited." In *Les Habitants du Toit du Monde: Études Recueillies en Hommage à Alexander W. Macdonald.* Samten Karmay and Philippe Sagant, eds. Recherches sur la Haute Asie 12. Nanterre: Société d'Ethnologie, pp. 75–109.

Stuart, Kevin, Banmadorji, and Huangchojia. 1995. "Mountain Gods and Trance Mediums: A Qinghai Tibetan Summer Festival." In *Asian Folklore Studies* 54(2), pp. 219–237.

Stuart, Kevin and Dpal-ldan-bkra-shis. 1998. "Perilous Novelties: The A-mdo Tibetan *klu-rol* Festival in Gling-rgyal Village." In *Anthropos* 93, pp. 31–53.

Sutherland, Gail Hinich. 1991. *The Disguises of the Demon: The Development of the Yakṣa in Hinduism and Buddhism.* Albany: SUNY Press.

Tenzin, Khempo Sangyay and Gomchen Oleshey. 1975. "The Nyingma Icons: A Collection of Line Drawings of 94 Deities and Divinities of Tibet." In *Kailash* 3(4), pp. 319–416.

Tenzin Samphel. 2008. "Les *bKa' Brgyad* – Sources Canoniques et Tradition de Nyang ral Nyi ma 'Od zer." In *Revue d'Etudes Tibétaines* 15, pp. 251–274.

Tewari, Ramesh Chandra. 1987. "Pre-Buddhist Elements in Himalayan Buddhism: The Institution of the Oracles." In *The Journal of the International Association of Buddhist Studies* 10(1), pp. 135–155.

Tibetan Academy of Social Sciences, ed. 2009. *Dpal ldan 'bras spungs dgon gyi dkar chag dri med dwangs gsal shel gyi me long*. Beijing: Krung go'i bod rig pa dpe skrun khang.

Toussaint, Gustave-Charles. 1933. *Le Dict de Padma: Padma thang yig, Ms. de Lithang*. Paris: Librarie Ernest Leroux.

Tucci, Giuseppe. 1965. "The Tibetan Tradition of Geography." In *Bulletin of Tibetology* 2(1), pp. 17–25.

[1949] 1999. *Tibetan Painted Scrolls*, 3 vols. Bangkok: SDI Publications.

Ugyen Pelgen. 2007. "Rituals and Pilgrimage Devoted to Aum Jo mo Re ma ti by the 'Brog pas of Me rag of Eastern Bhutan." In *Bhutan: Traditions and Changes. PIATS 2003: Tibetan Studies: Proceedings of the Tenth Seminar of the International Association for Tibetan Studies, Oxford, 2003*, vol. 5. John Ardussi and Françoise Pommaret, eds. Leiden: Brill, pp. 121–134.

Vargas-O'Bryan, Ivette. 2013. "Falling Rain, Reigning Power in Reptilian Affairs: The Balancing of Religion and the Environment," In *Charming Beauties and Frightful Beasts: Non-Human Animals in South Asian Myth, Ritual and Folklore*. Fabrizio M. Ferrari and Thomas Dähnhardt, eds. Sheffield: Equinox, pp. 99–114.

von Glahn, Richard. 2004. *The Sinister Way: The Divine and the Demonic in Chinese Religious Culture*. Berkeley: University of California Press.

Waddell, L. A. 1895. "The Tibetan House-Demon." In *Journal of the Anthropological Institute of Great Britain and Ireland* 24, pp. 39–41.

[1893] 1973. *Lamaism in Sikhim*. Delhi: Oriental Publishers.

Walter, Michael. 1996. "Scapula Cosmography and Divination in Tibet." In *Kailash* 18(3/4), pp. 107–114.

2009. *Buddhism and Empire: The Political and Religious Culture of Early Tibet*. Leiden: Brill.

Wangdu, Pasang and Hildegard Diemberger, trans. 2000. *dBa' bzhed: The Royal Narrative Concerning the Bringing of the Buddha's Doctrine to Tibet*. Vienna: Verlag der Österreichischen Akademie der Wissenschaften.

Watt, Jeff. 2019. "Tibetan Worldly Spirits, Sprites & Ogres." *Himalayan Art Resources*. www.himalayanart.org/search/set.cfm?setid=2554.

Williamson, Laila, and Serinity Young, eds. 2009. *Body and Spirit: Tibetan Medical Paintings*. New York: American Museum of Natural History

Willis, Janice. 1987. "Dakini: Some Comments on Its Nature and Meaning." In *Feminine Ground: Essays on Women in Tibet*. Janice Willis, ed. Ithica: Snow Lion, pp. 57–75.

Willson, Martin and Martin Brauen, eds. 2000. *Deities of Tibetan Buddhism: The Zürich Paintings of the Icons Worthwhile to See (Bris sku mthon ba don ldan)*. Boston: Wisdom Publications.

Wylie, Turrell. 1959. "A Standard System of Tibetan Transcription." In *Harvard Journal of Asiatic Studies* 22, pp. 261–267.

1962. *The Geography of Tibet According to the 'Dzam-Gling-Rgyas-Bshad*. Rome: Istituto Italiano per il Medio ed Estremo Oriente.

Yamamoto, Carl. 2012. *Vision and Violence: Lama Zhang and the Politics of Charisma in Twelfth-Century Tibet*. Leiden: Brill.

Acknowledgments

I dedicate this book to my parents, George and Wanda Bell, for all their love and tireless support.

Cambridge Elements ☰

Religion and Violence

James R. Lewis
University of Tromsø

James R. Lewis is Professor of Religious Studies at the
University of Tromsø, Norway and the author and editor of
a number of volumes, including *The Cambridge Companion to
Religion and Terrorism.*

Margo Kitts
Hawai'i Pacific University

Margo Kitts edits the *Journal of Religion and Violence* and is
Professor and Coordinator of Religious Studies and East-West
Classical Studies at Hawai'i Pacific University in Honolulu.

ABOUT THE SERIES

Violence motivated by religious beliefs has become all too common
in the years since the 9/11 attacks. Not surprisingly, interest in the
topic of religion and violence has grown substantially since then.
This Elements series on Religion and Violence addresses this new,
frontier topic in a series of c. fifty individual Elements. Collectively,
the volumes will examine a range of topics, including violence in
major world religious traditions, theories of religion and violence,
holy war, witch hunting, and human sacrifice, among others.

Cambridge Elements $\equiv$

Religion and Violence

ELEMENTS IN THE SERIES

The Problem of Job and the Problem of Evil
Espen Dahl

Islam and Violence
Khaleel Mohammed

Human Sacrifice: Archaeological Perspectives from around the World
Laerke Recht

Religious Culture and Violence in Traditional China
Barend ter Haar

Mormonism and Violence: The Battles of Zion
Patrick Q. Mason

Islam and Suicide Attacks
Pieter Nanninga

Tibetan Demonology
Christopher Bell

A full series listing is available at: www.cambridge.org/ERAV

Printed in the United States
By Bookmasters